How To Live A Christian Life

At Church, Work, Neighborhood, and Country

G. Michael Cocoris

© 2010, 2025 G. Michael Cocoris

All rights reserved. This publication may not be reproduced (in whole or in part, edited, or revised) in any way, form, or means, including, but not limited to electronic, mechanical, photocopying, recording or any kind of storage and retrieval system *for sale*, except for brief quotations in printed reviews, without the written permission of G. Michael Cocoris, 2016 Euclid #20, Santa Monica, CA 90405, michaelcocoris@gmail.com, or his appointed representatives. Permission is hereby granted, however, for the reproduction of the whole or parts of the whole without changing the content in any way for *free distribution*, provided all copies contain this copyright notice in its entirety. Permission is also granted to charge for the cost of copying.

Unless otherwise indicated all Scripture quotations are taken from the New King James Version ®, Copyright © 1979, 1980, 1982 by Thomas Nelson, Inc. Used by permission. All rights reserved.

Exterior and Interior design by John T. Cocoris

TABLE OF CONTENTS

Preface

Chapter 1 How To Be A Christian At Church 1

Chapter 2 How Not To Relate At Church 13

Chapter 3 How To Relate At Church 23

Chapter 4 How To Serve At Church 35

Chapter 5 How To Minister At Church 47

Chapter 6 How To Be Christ-Like At Church 63

Chapter 7 How To Be A Christian Boss 73

Chapter 8 How To Be A Christian Employee 83

Chapter 9 How To Be A Christian Neighbor 97

Chapter 10 How To Be A Christian Citizen 113

Bliopraphy 129

About The Author 133

PREFACE

The Bible is the greatest book on relationships ever written. It follows a pattern. First, it discusses our relationship with God and, after that, our relationships with other people. For example, when asked which commandment was the greatest, Jesus said, "You shall love the LORD your God with all your heart, with all your soul, and with all your mind. This is *the* first and greatest commandment. And *the* second *is* like it: 'You shall love your neighbor as yourself'" (Mt. 22:37-39). Then He added, "On these two commandments hang all the Law and the Prophets" (Mt. 22:40).

I explored what the New Testament says about our relationship with God in a study entitled *How to Live a Biblical Spiritual Life*. It explained how to live "alive to God." Under the title *The Road to the Ultimate in Marriage*, I expounded what the Scripture teaches concerning our family relationships. In addition to our relationship to the Lord and our family, the New Testament epistles deal with other relationships, such as our relationship to one another at church, our relationships at work, our relationships to our neighbors and our relationship to the government. I have elected to group these relationships together in this study called *How To Live The Christian Life*.

The word "Christian" only occurs three times in the New Testament. Luke records, "The disciples were first called Christians in Antioch" (Acts 11:26). Notice that the text says *disciples* were called Christians. In other words, those who were *following the Lord* began to be called "Christians." Moreover, "Christian" was not a name the disciples chose for themselves. It was a nickname given to them by others.

Bruce suggests that the pagans of Antioch gave the disciples this name because it was the name of the person about whom they were always talking. He adds they were the Christ-people, the Christians, just as the adherents of the Herod dynasty were called Herodians. Marshall uses the term "Christ-people" and says that it is likely that the name contained an element of ridicule (Acts 26:28; 1 Pet. 4:16). He adds Christians themselves preferred other names for themselves, such as "disciples, saints, and brothers."

Barclay explains, "The people of Antioch were famous for their facility in finding jesting nicknames. Later, the bearded Emperor Julian came to visit them and they christened him 'The Goat.' The termination *-iani* means *belonging to the party of*; for instance, *Caesariani* means *belonging to Caesar's party*. Christian means *these Christ-folk*. It was a contemptuous nickname, but the Christians took it and made it known to all the world. By their lives, they made it a name not of contempt but of respect and admiration and even wonder."

In the mouth of Agrippa (Acts 26:28), it is a term of reproach, like Nazarene (Rackham). Its use in 1 Peter 4:16 implies that it was being employed in an unfriendly way (Stibbs/Walls). Peter says no one suffering identified as a "Christ party" member should ever be ashamed. In recording how the Christians were made Nero's scapegoats in AD 64, Tacitus refers to them as "a class of people loathed for their vices, who were commonly styled Christians after Christ, who was executed by the procurator Pontius Pilate when Tiberius was emperor" (*Annals* sv 44).

Thus, the Christian life is Christ-like in relation *to others*. It assumes the believer is living a spiritual life. It focuses on how a spiritual-minded believer relates to others.

The distinguishing characteristic of Christians should be love. Jesus says, "By this, all will know that you are My disciples if you have love for one another" (Jn. 13:35). The way we love one another is that we minister to one another. Paul says, "For you, brethren, have been called to liberty; only do not use liberty as an opportunity for the flesh, but through love serve one another" (Gal. 5:13).

I am indebted to Teresa Rogers for proofreading this material. May the Lord use these truths from the Scripture to enrich your relationships with others.

G. Michael Cocoris
Santa Monica, CA

Chapter 1

How To Be A Christian At Church

When I was in college, a friend from my hometown came to see me with an urgent request. He told me that his father had just called to tell him, "They are about to crucify your father and you need to get home as soon as possible." My friend did not have a car, but I did. He wanted to know if we could use my car to go home immediately. Of course, I said, "Yes." In record time, we drove 400 miles to Pensacola, Florida.

My friend's father was a pastor of a large church with a school. The principal of the school accused him of mishandling the financial affairs with the insinuation that he had taken money. I had reason to believe that was false, but a congregational meeting had been called to deal with the issue.

I was a young Christian. As I recall, I had never been to a church business meeting. I sat on the back row of a large sanctuary to observe the proceedings. The meeting began orderly enough but quickly degenerated. There were angry tones, interruptions, and raised voices. I remember feeling that the meeting was getting out of hand. It got so bad I thought a fight was going to break out and I decided that if it did, I would have to call the police.

After several hours of that, the meeting ended without outside intervention. Because of that meeting, the pastor resigned, the church split, and, as I recall, the school eventually closed.

Since that experience many years ago, I have heard horror stories of unchristian-like conduct at church. I have heard of business meetings that did erupt into fights, of church members doing and saying ungodly things, and of people attending the same church without speaking to each other for years!

On her first Sunday in First Baptist Church, West Lafayette, Ohio, Pauline Rice heard the pastor read a list of those he was expelling from the church. They were present and stood up to shout him down. Two men ended up in a fistfight on the church lawn (told by Rev. David Holwick, Pastor of First Baptist Church West Lafayette, Ohio, in a sermon on September 26, 1982).

I dare say that in every church, every week, Christians act toward one another in an unchristian-like manner. All of this provokes me to ask, "How are Christians supposed to be Christians at church?"

One New Testament book focuses on the church more than any other. Some suggest that the subject of Ephesians is the church. In my opinion, that is not precisely correct, but there is no doubt that Ephesians has a great deal to say about the church. A critical passage discusses how to be a Christian at church.

Your Calling

Paul begins the last half of Ephesians with the exhortation, "I, therefore, the prisoner of the Lord, beseech you to have a walk worthy of the calling with which you were called" (Eph. 4:1). The word "therefore" indicates this admonition is based on Ephesians 1-3.

Our Calling God has called us to Himself and to be part of His church. We were spiritually dead in sin (Eph. 2:1-3), separated from God and His family (Eph. 2:11, 12). God regenerated us (Eph. 2:4-6), reconciled us to Himself and other believers (Eph. 2:13-18), and revealed His eternal plan and purpose to us (Eph. 1:9, 10; 3:2-6). We are in Christ, in the heavenlies and in the church. That's our calling.

Our Conduct Now, God asks us to walk worthy of that calling. The word "walk" is a metaphor for living, for conduct. Our calling should determine our conduct. As believers, we should walk worthy of our calling. Paul urges us to do this as a prisoner of the Lord. If he could endure imprisonment for the sake of the Lord's work, we should be able to conduct our lives worthy of the Lord outside of jail.

How is that done? What are the characteristics of a worthy walk? Technically, the remainder of Ephesians answers that question, but a few general characteristics are given at the beginning of this discussion (Eph. 4:1-3).

Your Conduct

Humility and Gentleness For example, Paul says, "With all lowliness and gentleness" (Eph. 4:2a). The Greek word translated "lowliness" means "lowliness of mind, humility." Humility is not the way you speak or act; it is lowliness of *mind*; it is the way you *think*. It is not being modest; it is a frame of mind that is a realistic view of oneself. Chrysostom says humility is the foundation of all virtues. McGee calls it "The flagship of all Christian virtues."

Humility is the opposite of pride. Westcott says, "Humility is a thankful sense of dependence upon God as opposed to pride and self-confidence." Hodge says it is the "opposite not only of self-complacency and self-conceit, but also of the self-exultation, and setting oneself up to attract the honor which comes from men." Eadie says it stands further from "haughtiness, arrogance, and conceit, which is produced by the right view of ourselves, and our relationship to Christ and to that glory to which we are called."

The way to be a Christian at church is to be a Christian with humility. A pastor friend told me of a church leader who was instrumental in starting a church. For years, he was one of its prominent leaders. Then, he moved to another city. After his departure, the church grew even larger. Sometime later, the man who started the church moved back and once again attended the church he helped start. Most of the people did not know him because they were new. When the time came for the election of officers, he was asked to be an alternate since he was not well known. He refused. When asked, "Why?" He said, "I started this church." That is the attitude of pride, which says, "Do you know who I am?"

In the Greek text, lowliness and gentleness are tied together with one preposition ("with"), suggesting that "meekness" is a phase of "humility" (Eadie). "Gentleness" is the Greek word "meek," which, contrary to popular opinion, is not weakness. It is strength under control. The Greeks used the word for a soothing medicine, a controlled horse, and a soft wind, each of which pictures controlled power. Moses (Num. 12:3) and Christ (Mt. 11:29) are the two outstanding examples of meekness in the Scripture. Neither was weak; both were gentle.

Westcott states, "Meekness is a consideration for others, even under provocation, as opposed to self-assertion." Hodge says it is "softness and gentleness, which when united with strength is one of the loveliest attributes of our nature." He describes meekness as "that unresisting, uncomplaining disposition of mind which enables us to bear without irritation or resentment the faults and injuries of others. It is the disposition of which the lamb, dumb before the shearers, is the symbol and which is one of the most wonderful of all virtues of the Son of God. The most exalted of all beings was the gentlest."

Meekness can be seen in the soft answer, which turns away wrath (Prov. 15:1). Jesus Christ was meek, an attitude He exhibited in that He was slow to take offense. Matthew records that Jesus was meek (Mt. 11:29) and tells this story in the next chapter. Jesus Christ was once charged with being of the devil. That, of course, was not true. It was a lie, but imagine how the Son of God must have felt being called the son of Beelzebub. Surely, He felt the sting of the accusation, but He did not revile the people who accused Him. He gently and meekly answered them.

Patience and Forbearance Paul says that the worthy walk is to be accomplished "with longsuffering" (Eph. 4:2a). The Greek word translated "longsuffering" is made up of two words: "long" plus "wrath" (that is, passion or hot temper). It is the opposite of being short-tempered; it is being long-tempered. It is the opposite of irritability, enabling people to bear with those who oppose them and who, in any way, do them an injustice (Eadie). Patience is a good translation. It has particular reference to being patient with people.

John Wesley's father told his mother, "I marvel at your patience! You have told that child the same thing twenty times." Susanna Wesley replied, "Had I spoken the matter only nineteen times, I should have lost all my labor."

At this point in the passage, Paul adds two participial phrases: "bearing one another in love" (Eph. 4:2c) and "endeavoring to keep the unity of the Spirit in the bond of peace" (Eph. 4:3). These phrases probably modify all three virtues mentioned in Ephesians 4:1-3, namely humility, meekness, and patience, but the first one particularly seems to be a further development of the last virtue, patience. That is the case in Colossians 3:12-13, where "bearing one another" modifies "longsuffering."

The Greek word translated "bearing" means "to hold up, to bear with, endure." It also means "to bear with, as in "to listen to" (A-S; see also Col. 3:13). In Acts 18:14, it means "to listen to." Saying it means "to restrain oneself," Hodge says it is restraining oneself in reference to each other in love.

Forbearance implies that the other person is being particularly difficult. Westcott comments on this passage, "Forbearing one another in the case of real grievances." Eadie says something similar: "To hold oneself up until the provocation is past." Erdman agrees, "This (longsuffering) is to be expressed in action by mutual forbearance which indicates the ability to continue to love, even when conscious of faults which displease and offend."

Patience bears with people in love. Love is the sphere in which it is possible to forbear people patiently. Love suffers long (1 Cor. 13:4). It also bears all things (1 Cor. 13:7). F. F. Bruce has said, "Mutual patience and forbearance are not graces which come readily or naturally, but those who have learned to appreciate gratefully God's patience and forbearance with them will desire to show the same attitude to others. Paul is, in effect, urging his readers to cultivate the graces that were seen in perfection in Christ and to love one another as He had loved them."

Speaking to our pastor's group, Dallas Willard, a Christian author who teaches philosophy at USC, said that most look at 1 Corinthians 13 and think, this is what I have to do. That is not what Paul is saying. Paul is saying this is what love does. If you want to be like that, be loving!

Unity The second participial phrase is "endeavoring to keep the unity of the Spirit in the bond of peace" (Eph. 4:3). This may be a further elaboration on patience, forbearance, or the three main virtues of the passage: humility, meekness, and patience.

The Holy Spirit has already produced unity. Jews and Gentiles, two very diverse groups, have been reconciled to God and to each other in one new body (Eph. 2:15, 16). Unity has been established; now, it must be maintained.

Paul urges believers to "endeavor to keep" the unity that already exists. The word Greek translated "endeavor" means "to make haste, hence, to be zealous or eager, to give diligence." Clearly, Paul is urging that effort and energy be put forth to keep what has been established. The Greek word "keep" means "to watch over, guard, keep, preserve." Believers do not manufacture unity; they guard it. Believers cannot create unity in the church; God has already done that. The believer can only destroy it. Believers either maintain unity or mess it up.

This is a critical issue. "These six *things* the LORD hates, Yes, seven *are* an abomination to Him: A proud look, a lying tongue, hands that shed innocent blood, a heart that devises wicked plans, feet that are swift in running to evil, a false witness *who* speaks lies, and one who sows discord among brethren" (Prov. 6:16-19). The Lord hates those who sow discord.

Peace How does a believer maintain unity? The last phrase in verse 3 says, "in the bond of peace." As Hohner puts it: "Concern for peace will mean that Christians will lovingly tolerate each other, even when they have differences." "The peace that results from love, humility, meekness, and mutual forbearance is essential to the union and communion of the members of Christ the body" (Hodge). Believers have peace with God (Eph. 2:16-17) and with each other (Eph. 2:14-15). So, they should seek peace among themselves (Eph. 4:1; Jas. 3:17). Peace is the tranquility that ought to reign in the church (Eadie).

"When the graces of verse 2 are cultivated, the unity of the Spirit is preserved" (Bruce). The axiom of Rupertus Meldenius, a Lutheran theologian, set down in his treatise *Paraenesis Votiva Pro Pace Ecclesia* (1626)—so often quoted by Richard Baxter that it is frequently taken to be his own—was, "Let there be unity in things necessary, in things unnecessary liberty, in all things charity."

The motto of the Apollo 11 flight was, "We come in peace for all mankind." That motto was on the plaque deposited on the face of the moon on the Sea of Tranquility by Neil Armstrong and Buzz Aldrin. If believers come in peace, there will be a sea of tranquility.

Summary: A walk worthy of our calling to Christ in the church is characterized by humility, meekness, patience, and seeking to maintain unity through peace. The way to be a Christian at church is to be Christ-like.

Jesus Christ, the first and foremost in heaven, humbled Himself (Phil. 2:8), meekly ministered (Mt. 11:29), and patiently endured His adversaries and the adversity of His trial and crucifixion. Paul mentions the attitude of Christ and exhorts the Philippians to be like-minded (Phil. 2:5), and more specifically, "Let nothing be done through selfish ambition or conceit, but in lowliness of mind let each esteem others better than himself" (Phil. 2:3), and still further, "being of one accord, of one mind" (Phil. 2:2). Jesus was humble, meek, and patient. Therefore, we who know Him should adopt the same attitude so we can live a life worthy of Him and live a life of harmony and unity in the church. This sometimes means 1) biting our tongue when we wish to speak out, 2) not always demanding our way but joyfully following the will of the majority, 3) avoiding at all costs gossip and cutting, critical remarks, 4) avoiding the spread of rumors, and 5) eliminating negative, cursory remarks from our conversation.

Everything in this passage is the opposite of a heady, high-minded, haughty, harsh, hostile, hateful lifestyle. It is the antithesis of the attitude of a world that says, "Me first, me above others, me ahead of the pack."

We do not live like that, do we? Paul "enforces the cultivation of these graces, the possession of which is indispensable to the harmony of the church: for the opposite vices—pride, irascibility, inpatient querulousness—all tend towards strife and disruption" (Eadie). As someone has said, "Some churches can't buy a bus, paint a bathroom, plan a promotion, schedule a revival, or take a special offering without fighting and squabbling about it. Every church seems to have two or three such people who are always questioning what's going on, criticizing the leadership, and demanding explanations for actions."

Why do we not live in harmony and unity in church? We live by how we think and we work against each other. Two men rode a bicycle built for two when they reached a big steep hill. It took a great deal of struggle for the men to complete what proved to be a very stiff climb. When they got to the top, the man in front turned to the other and said, "Boy, that sure was a hard climb. The fellow in back replied, "Yes, and if I hadn't kept the brakes on all the way, we would certainly have rolled down backward."

It comes down to pride. "By pride comes nothing but strife, but with the well-advised *is* wisdom" (Prov. 13:10). "When pride comes, then comes shame; but with the humble *is* wisdom" (Prov. 11:2).

A visitor to a mental hospital was astonished to note that only three guards were watching over 100 dangerous inmates. He asked his guide, "Don't you fear these people will overpower the guards and escape?" "No," was the reply. "Lunatics never unite." Lunatics do not unite; Christ-like believers do.

During the World Series, when the San Francisco Giants' starting lineup was announced, each player jogged to the first baseline, gave a high five or, shook hands with one another, and got in line. When their star player, Barry Bonds, was introduced, he jogged to his spot in line, avoiding the other players. When you think about a team, it takes all 25 players on a baseball team to win or lose. Bonds may have been the best hitter in baseball, but he was not the only player on the team.

During a Super Bowl, the New England Patriots didn't announce their star players so they could run onto the field to the cheering crowd. Instead, the *team* was announced and they all ran onto the field together. To be a Christian at church, remember that you are part of a team and behave accordingly.

Be of one mind. Unity is not uniformity. It does not mean that everyone has the same opinion about everything. It means having the same thoughts and feelings about a particular issue, a "common interest" (Stibbs/Walls). Believers should have the mind of Christ (Phil. 2:5), who submitted to serve. "Unity does not mean uniformity; it means cooperation in the midst of diversity" (Wiersbe). It is "thinking harmoniously" (Grudem). Believers should be united in purpose, objectives, and goals. This is a recurring theme in the New Testament (Rom. 12:16; 2 Cor. 13:11; Phil. 2:2; also 1 Cor. 1:10; Eph. 4:3; Phil. 1:27; 3:15).

Chapter 2

How To Not Relate At Church

Relating to one another is a problem—a huge problem. The German philosopher Schopenhauer compared the human race to a bunch of porcupines huddling together on a cold winter's night. He said, "The colder it gets outside, the more we huddle together for warmth, but the closer we get to one another, the more we hurt one another with our sharp quills. And in the lonely night of earth's winter, eventually, we begin to drift apart and wander out on our own and freeze to death in our loneliness." It is like an older fellow I once heard say, "Women! You can't live with'm and you can't live without'm."

How can we relate to one another without hurting one another or getting hurt by one another? It can be done.

As we have seen, God expects believers to live in harmony with one another. It takes humility, meekness, patience, forbearance, and an effort to maintain unity. So, it can be done. Beyond those general ideas, the New Testament gives more specific instructions for relating to one another. These directives are given to believers concerning how to relate to one another in church, but the church is the lab where we learn how to do what we should do outside the lab.

These specific instructions are in the expression "one another." The Greek word translated "one another" is a reciprocal pronoun, which means "one another, mutually." In the New Testament, it is used just shy of 100 times. In many of those occurrences, it is used for nothing more than speaking to one another (Mk. 4:41; Lk. 6:11; Jn. 4:33). It is also used in ways no one should ever relate to one another, such as betraying one another (Mt. 24:10), hating one another (Mt. 24:10; Titus 3:3), and doing wrong to one another (Acts 7:26).

In the last chapter, we looked at forbearance and unity. Those two ideas are given with the expression "one another." Paul says, "Bearing with one another in love" (Eph. 4:1-3; Col. 3:13) and "Be of the same mind toward one another" (Rom. 12:16; 15:5; 1 Pet. 3:8). The following is a look at some of the other ways the phrase "one another" is used in the epistles to inform believers about how they are to relate to one another, especially in church.

Our Connection

The place to begin is with the concept that we are "members of one another." Paul says that twice (Rom. 12:5; Eph. 4:25). The metaphor of being members of one of another is more completely developed in 1 Corinthians 12:12-27, where the illustration is that of the physical body. Believers are connected to one another as the members of our physical body are connected to one another.

Believers are all members of the same spiritual body, intimately united to each other with Christ as the head. "The relation of believers to each other is far more intimate than between the members of an external organization, whether civil or ecclesiastical. It is analogous to the mutual relationship of the members of the same body, animated by one soul" (Hodge on Rom. 12:5).

Since we are members of one another, there are things we should not do, and there are things we should do.

What Not to Do

Among believers, "one another" is used of things they are not to do to one another. These are ways of how *not* to relate to one another.

Do Not Lie to One Another Paul lists five sins that we are to put off: "But now you must put off these: anger, wrath, malice, blasphemy, filthy language out of your mouth" (Col. 3:8). Then he singles out one sin: "Do not lie to one another" (Col. 3:9). The special treatment of this sin makes its condemnation more emphatic. To lie is to tell a deliberate untruth, to distort the truth by only revealing part of it, or to exaggerate it. Many believers think nothing of stretching the truth by telling a white lie.

Lying prevents intimate relationships and often destroys relationships. A simple example is lying on a job application. Lying on a job application is grounds for termination.

Do Not Judge One Another Paul says, "For we shall all stand before the judgment seat of Christ. For it is written: As I live, says the Lord, every knee shall bow to Me, and every tongue shall confess to God. So then, each of us shall give an account of himself to God. Therefore, let us not judge one another anymore, but rather resolve this, not to put a stumbling block or a cause to fall in our brother's way" (Rom. 14:10-13). In this passage, Paul discusses doubtful things, that is, things that are *not* morally wrong, but some believe that those immoral things *are* wrong. For example, some claim going to the movies is wrong. Paul is saying that because God is the judge, we should not judge others concerning amoral things. If you want to judge, judge that you will not cause a brother to stumble. Don't pass judgment on your brother's decisions but on your own.

There is a proper and improper judging. On the one hand, the Scripture commands us to judge (1 Cor. 6:2-4). On the other hand, Jesus said, "Judge not" (Mt. 7:1). It sounds like Jesus is prohibiting all judging. Is He saying that being a judge in a talent contest is wrong? Is it sinful to evaluate job applicants? No. Jesus is not forbidding all judgment. Later in the passage, He said to judge people's character (Mt. 7:6) and to beware of prophets (Mt. 7:15), which involves judging.

Scripture commands proper judgment and forbids improper judgment. Proper judgment includes an appropriate judge, standard, and case. In other words, you can judge when it is your responsibility to judge, when you use a proper measurement (Scripture), and you have evidence. Believers are to discern the difference between truth and error in doctrine and distinguish between good and evil in deportment.

Improper judgment kills relationships. Usually, the falsely accused person withdraws from the relationship. The habitually false accusers almost always do not have many, if any, relationships, and certainly not intimate ones.

Do not Speak Evil of One Another James says, "Do not speak evil of one another, brethren. He who speaks evil of a brother and judges his brother, speaks evil of the law and judges the law" (Jas. 4:11). The Greek phrase "speak evil" means "to speak down." This word describes many kinds of harmful speech, including slander. Tyndale translated "speaking evil" as "backbite." The corresponding adjective in Romans 1:30 is rendered "backbiters." This same word is used twice in 1 Peter of the slander and misrepresentation, which Christians often suffered at the hands of non-Christians (1 Pet. 2:12, 3:16). Those who speak evil of others perceive themselves to be above others, which is an attitude of pride. James has just said believers are to be humble (Jas. 4:10).

I enjoy humor. As a young man, even as a teenager in high school, I loved to tell jokes. I collected them. Over the years, I have told fewer and fewer jokes because I began to realize that a great deal of humor is a putdown. I still enjoy humor and telling jokes, but I am much more sensitive to the "put down."

The "put down" is a shovel that digs the grave of relationships. It is so powerful that it will devastate and destroy a marriage. For example, "If you do not stop nagging me," yelled the golfer to his wife, "You are going to drive me out of my mind." To which she replied, "That would not be a drive. That's more like a gimme putt."

Do Not Grumble Against One Another James writes, "Do not grumble against one another, brethren" (Jas. 5:9a). The Greek word translated "grumble" means "to groan." In this verse, it has the idea of complaining, criticizing, and fault-finding.

Do Not Provoke One Another, Envy One Another "Let us not become conceited, provoking one another, envying one another" (Gal. 5:26). The Greek word rendered "provoking" means "challenge." Believers are not to challenge one another to a contest or combat. Believers are not in competition with one another. Neither are they to envy one another. The "haves" challenge. The "have nots" envy.

Do Not Bite and Devour One Another Paul exhorts, "But if you bite and devour one another, beware lest you be consumed by one another!" (Gal. 5:15). Paul pictures believers biting, gulping, and swallowing each other. Imagine two snakes eating each other's tail, slowly consuming each other. That is the picture! That's what Galatians did to each other over the controversy of liberty from the Mosaic Law. Without love (Gal. 5:14), believers destroy each other.

Summary: Because we are connected to one another in one body, we should not hurt one another by how we treat one another, especially by how we speak.

This is not about people who get their feelings hurt at the least little thing. It is about doing things that would hurt anyone. Rather than doing all of these negative things to each other, we should relate to each other in many positive ways. The next chapter explores those concepts in detail, but two more general principles serve as a conclusion to this discussion and an introduction to the next discussion.

Forgive One Another Paul tells believers to "be kind to one another, tenderhearted, forgiving one another, just as God in Christ forgave you" (Eph. 4:32). Because humans are sinful and, therefore, imperfect creatures, there cannot be intimate relationships without forgiveness. Forgiveness is not a feeling, faking a smile, or forgetting what happened.

The Greek word translated "forgiveness" means "to send away." What is sent away is, "Let all bitterness, wrath, anger, clamor, and evil speaking be put away from you, with all malice. And be kind to one another, tenderhearted, forgiving one another, just as God in Christ forgave you" (Eph. 4:31-32). Forgiveness, then, is turning loose and letting go of the anger, resentment, speaking against, and desire to punish those who have offended you. A pastor friend says forgiveness involves not repeating the offense to yourself repeatedly, not reminding the offender of the offense, and not repeating the offense to others.

Receive One Another Paul exhorts, "Therefore receive one another just as Christ also received us, to the glory of God (Rom. 15:7). This exhortation is the conclusion received us, to the glory of God (Rom. 15:7). This exhortation is the conclusion ("therefore") of the discussion of doubtful things begun in Romans 14:1 where Paul launched the subject with the command to "receive."

Paul began the discussion by saying, "Receive one who is weak in the faith, but not to disputes over doubtful things" (Rom. 14:1). The strong are to "receive" the weak. The strong have trusted Christ and believed God about other things, such as all food is clean if received with thanksgiving (1 Tim. 4:4, 5). The weak who have faith in Christ but are weak in that they believe they should only eat vegetables (Rom. 14:2). Doubtful things, then, are everyday things not intrinsically sinful, but some believers think that they are.

The Greek word translated "dispute" refers to judging or quarreling. The word rendered "doubtful things" means "thought, reasoning." The strong are to receive the weak in full fellowship as a brother without judging or quarreling with the individual's opinions. In this context, "to receive" means "to accept as a brother." Paul concludes, "Let not him who eats despise him who does not eat and let not him who does not eat judge him who eats; for God has received him" (Rom. 14:3). The strong are not to "despise" the weak. The Greek word translated "despise" means "to set at naught, treat with contempt." On the other hand, the weak are not to judge the strong as though God had not accepted them, for God receives meat eaters without condemning what they eat. Love dictates that believers receive each other and not judge each other concerning doubtful, debatable things.

Hence, Paul urged the strong and weak to receive one another (14:13; 15:7). He adds, "Just as Christ also received us, to the glory of God" (Rom. 15:7). Christ had accepted both the strong and the weak (14:3, 6, 15) and that glorified God. Likewise, we should accept one another to reflect God's grace. Since Christ has been gracious to us to the glory of God, we should be gracious to one another to God's glory.

Do Good to One Another Paul says, "See that no one renders evil for evil to anyone, but always pursue that which is good both with yourselves and for all" (1 Thess. 5:15). In the Greek text, the phrase "with yourselves" is the Greek word for "one another." If someone hurts a believer, that believer is not to retaliate in kind, but Paul does not stop there. Not only should the believers not do evil, but they should also always pursue good.

The Greek word translated "good" has the idea of being beneficial or helpful. It is not enough to decide not to retaliate. True righteousness goes further and says, "I will do something good for that person." So, when hurt or harmed, don't hurt back; instead, help.

The law of retaliation demands an eye for an eye, a tooth for a tooth, and a life for a life. That is justice. God is not only just. He is also gracious. Whereas the Old Testament includes the concept of an eye for an eye, the New Testament ideal is to bless or benefit those who curse you. Believers should strive to be like their gracious heavenly Father.

A homeless man in England who was hungry. As he wandered around looking for food, he stumbled upon a tavern and thought, "Maybe they have leftovers they would give me." Instead of going inside, he went to the back door and knocked. A woman came to the door. When he said he was without a job and asked for something to eat, she exploded, "You lazy good-for-nothing bum, why don't you get a job?" After listening to her rail on him, he apologized for disturbing her and left. As he left, he noticed the tavern's name was "Saint George and the Dragon." He immediately went to the rear door again and knocked. When the same woman came to the door again, he said, "May I speak to Saint George?"

There is a dragon in us. The Bible calls it the flesh. If you have trusted Jesus Christ for the gift of eternal life, you are a saint capable of being godly. The way not to treat people is to send the dragon to the door; instead, send the saintly side of you.

Chapter 3

How To Relate At Church

Relating to one another is one of the problems in life. Growing up, we have problems with our parents. We struggle with our siblings. We have trouble getting along with at least one or two individuals at school. Conflicts at work are common. The one place where people ought to be able to get along with one another is at church. Unfortunately, there are often as many difficulties getting along with people at church as at home, school, and work.

We need instruction concerning relating to one another. The New Testament gives us information about how to relate to one another at church. Those principles apply to all relationships. How, then, are we to relate to one another at church? Relationships at church begin with the concept that we are "members of one another" (Rom. 12:5; Eph. 4:25). At least part of the answer lies in the statements containing the expression "one another."

The General Principles

Love One Another Jesus said that He gave us a new commandment that we *love one another* (Jn. 13:34). This command is given repeatedly in the New Testament (see Jn. 13:35; 15:12; 17; 1

Thess. 3:12; 4:9; 2 Thess. 1:3; 1 Pet. 1:22; 4:8; 1 Jn. 3:11, 23; 4:7, 11; 12; 2 Jn. 5). To that list should be added what Paul said in Romans chapter 12, namely, "Be kindly affectionate to one another with brotherly love, in honor giving preference to one another" (Rom. 12:10).

There are four Greek words for love: 1) *agape*, 2) *philia*, 3) *storge*, and 4) *eros*. *Agape* is an act of the will whereby one seeks the highest good of another. *Philia* means looking at someone with affectionate regard. It was used for the love of friends. *Storge* refers to family affection. *Eros* was the word for physical love.

Two of the four Greek words for love appear in the New Testament. Another occurs in a compound form. *Agape* is used in Romans 12:9. True love is the one that seeks the highest good for the one loved. *Philia* is used in Romans 12:10, where it is translated "kindly affectionate." True love, which seeks the highest good for others, views another believer with affectionate regard. The third Greek word for love is not used in the New Testament by itself, but in compound form, which includes it, is used in Romans 12:10, where it is translated "brotherly love." In other words, true love (Rom. 12:9) looks at believers with affectionate regard (Rom. 12:10) because believers are members of the same family (Rom. 12:10). The fourth word is not used in the New Testament in any form (Barclay, *More New Testament Words*, pp. 11-15).

The point of Romans 12:10 is believers should love each other with the same sincerity and tenderness as they do a near and dear relative (Hodge). Tender and intimate affection between family members is appropriate among believers.

More specifically, they should "in honor" give preference to one another (Rom. 12:10). Believers can genuinely love one another by preferring each other. Rather than seeking honor for oneself, true love gives the place of honor to others. Paul says, "*Let* nothing *be done* through selfish ambition or conceit, but in lowliness of mind let each esteem others better than himself" (Phil. 2:3).

The greatest description of love in literature is in 1 Corinthians 13. It teaches us how loves behaves.

HOW LOVE BEHAVES

1. Love suffers long. Love is patient with people. It patiently bears provocation and injuries. It is slow to take offense, get angry, or be aroused to resentment.
2. Love is kind. Love is good-natured and does good things. It is good, serviceable, useful, gracious, bestowing benefits on others. It never says anything unkind.
3. Love is not envy. Love is not jealous. It is not displeased at the position or possessions of others.
4. Love does not parade itself. Love does not brag. It does not draw attention to itself.
5. Love is not puffed up. Love is not proud. It does not have a superior attitude.
6. Love does not behave rudely. Love does not act unbecomingly. It has good manners and makes you feel comfortable. It is not rude.

7. Love does not seek its own. Love is not self-seeking; it seeks the benefits of others. It does not trade being right for another person's feelings.
8. Love is not provoked. Love is not easily aroused to anger. It is not ready to take offense. It's not touchy (Phillips). It is not easily irritated.
9. Love thinks no evil. Love does not register wrongs. It does not keep books on insults or injuries. Love forgives.
10. Love does not rejoice in iniquity. Love does not rejoice over another's fault. It is not gleeful over another's moral downfall.
11. Love rejoices in the truth. Love rejoices when truth triumphs.
12. Love bears all things. Love endures the irritation of others.
13. Love believes all things. Love looks at facts, not rumors. It gives the benefit of the doubt. It prefers to err in the direction of trusting too much than too little.
14. Love hopes all things. Love hopes for the best, even when there is a present failure. Love expects future victory.
15. Love endures all things. It patiently endures circumstances, trouble, and affliction. It remains steadfast in the face of unpleasant circumstances.

The essence of these characteristics of love is selflessness. For example, love is not jealous, a characteristic that thinks of self and not others. An illustration is in 1 Corinthians 11, where Paul says, "Therefore, my brethren, when you come together to eat, *wait for one another"* (1 Cor. 11:33).

To say the same thing another way, love gives preference to others. The Danish paddlers were leading during the world championship marathon tandem kayak race in Copenhagen when their rudder was damaged. The British paddlers, who were in second place, stopped to help the Danes fix it. The Danes defeated the British by one second in an event that lasted nearly three hours. The British kayakers, however, won what many regard as the highest honor in sports. They received the Pierre de Coubertin International Fair Play Trophy. The trophy is named for the founder of the modern Olympic Games and is awarded annually to people in sports who have demonstrated nobility of spirit. It is big news in Europe but has not been recognized much in the United States.

The first Fair Play Trophy went to an Italian bobsledder named Eugenio Monti for a gesture that exhibited a touch of class. Monti was the leader in the two-man bobsled event at the 1964 Innsbruck Olympics after his final run. The only one given a chance to beat him was Tony Nash of Great Britain. As Nash and his teammate prepared for their final run, they discovered that a critical bolt on their sled had snapped at the last moment. Monti was informed of the problem and immediately took the corresponding bolt from his sled and sent it to Nash. Nash fixed his sled, came hurtling down the course to set a record and won the gold medal (*Bits and Pieces*, October 15, 1992, pp. 4-6).

The trophy has been given to a Hungarian tennis player who pleaded with officials to give his opponent more time to recover from a cramp and to a high school basketball coach who forfeited the Georgia (US) state championship after he found out that one of his players was scholastically ineligible.

Speak the Truth In Colossians, Paul says not to lie to one another. In Ephesians, he says, "Therefore, putting away lying, let each one *of you* speak truth with his neighbor, for we are members of one another" (Eph. 4:25). He does not use the expression "one another" in Ephesians, but since that is the point in Colossians and a very important issue in all relationships, it needs to be part of how to relate to one another.

Love and speaking the truth are the two fundamental principles of all relationships. The way to relate is to have a loving, honest interaction with another person.

The Specifics

Greet One Another In the New Testament, believers are told to greet one another five times. Paul says they are to greet one another with a holy kiss (Rom. 16:16; 1 Cor. 16:20; 2 Cor. 13:12; 1 Thess. 5:26). This kiss was to be holy; it has no romantic overtones. Peter says they are to greet one another with a kiss of love (1 Pet. 5:14). This kiss expresses love and affection.

In ancient times, men kissed men on the cheek, and women kissed women. Today, people greet each other with spoken words, such as, "Hi, how are you?" with a handshake and brief embrace. Believers are to greet one another with a holy and affectionate touch.

How To Relate At Church

Psychologists tell us that people need to be touched. Studies have shown that cuddled infants gained weight faster and were healthier than those not. "It is much harder to get mad at someone you have just hugged or kissed, and it is much easier to feel accepted in a fellowship which has given such a warm welcome!" (Grudem on 1 Pet. 5:14).

Sing to One Another Paul says, "Be filled with the Spirit, speaking to one another in psalms and hymns and spiritual songs, singing and making melody in your heart to the Lord, giving thanks always for all things to God the Father in the name of our Lord Jesus Christ" (Eph. 5:18-20) and "teaching and admonishing one another in psalms and hymns and spiritual songs, singing with grace in your hearts to the Lord (Col. 3:9-16). According to these verses, we speak to one another, teach one another, and admonish one another when we sing.

I cannot sing. I do not have an ear for music. When the notes go up, I go too high up. When the notes go down, I go too far down, but I love music, and I sing when I am alone and am sure no one can hear me. On one occasion, I had one piece of bad news after another. The news was not about me directly; it all involved other people. As I thought about what was happening, I was not necessarily discouraged, but I was down emotionally. So, I did two things. I prayed and I began to sing. What I was singing began to speak to me. I was instructed and inspired by what I was singing. I was amazed at how quickly my spirits rose. I have had that happen in church. Listening to a church full of people sing speaks emotionally, teaches, and admonishes you and others.

Fellowship with One Another John says, "If we walk in the light as He is in the light, we have fellowship with one another, and the blood of Jesus Christ His Son cleanses us from all sin" (1 Jn. 1:7). Luke records that after 3000 got saved on the day of Pentecost, "they continued steadfastly in the apostles' doctrine and fellowship, in the breaking of bread, and in prayers" (Acts 2:42). The Greek word translated "fellowship" means "fellowship, communion." The idea is "sharing." There is an often-repeated statement that fellowship is two fellows in a ship. Clever, but not exactly the concept. Those two fellows could not speak to each other, be angry at each other, or fight with each other, none of which is fellowship. Fellowship is sharing your thoughts and heart with someone else.

Anyone who goes to church and does not fellowship with people does not understand the New Testament concept of church. Going to church just for the music or to hear the message is not "church." It is self-absorption.

We have a pot-luck lunch at our church on every Sunday of every month. I believe it is one of the most important things we do. It is the one thing we do that is designed for fellowship.

Pray for One Another James says, "Confess *your* trespasses to one another, and pray for one another, that you may be healed. The effective, fervent prayer of a righteous man avails much" (Jas. 5:16). In my opinion, this is a special case, not a general principle. This passage is about believers who are in conflict with each other (Jas. 4:1-2), and, as a result, they are physically ill (Jas. 5:14). The sickness here is due to sin (1 Cor. 11:30). In that context, James tells them to confess their faults and pray for one another to be healed. Assumed but not stated, they should also forgive one another (Eph. 4:32; Col. 3:13).

At the same time, many passages indicate that we should pray for one another. Samuel said, "Moreover, as for me, far be it from me that I should sin against the Lord in ceasing to pray for you" (1 Sam. 12:23).

Care for One Another Paul writes, "God composed the body, having given greater honor to that part which lacks it, that there should be no schism in the body, but that the members should have the same *care for one another*. And if one member suffers, all the members suffer with it; or if one member is honored, all the members rejoice with it" (1 Cor. 12:24-26). A sign on a church marquee read, "We care about you. Sunday, 10 am only."

Mamie Adams always went to a branch post office in her town because the postal employees there were friendly. She went there to buy stamps just before Christmas one year and the lines were particularly long. Someone pointed out that there was no need to wait in line because there was a stamp machine in the lobby. "I know," said Mamie, "but the machine won't ask me about my arthritis" (*Bits and Pieces*, December 1989, p. 2).

Be Compassionate for One Another Peter says, "Finally, all *of you be* of one mind, having compassion for one another love as brothers, be tenderhearted, be courteous" (1 Pet. 3:8). The Greek word translated "compassion" is a compound word (it combines "suffer" and "with") that means "affected by like feelings, sympathetic." It is the Greek word from which we get our word "sympathetic." It denotes "sharing the experience of another" (Moulton and Milligan), and "suffering together" (Stibbs/Walls). Compassionate people suffer together with others (Rom. 12:15). Here is the test. Paul exhorts us to "rejoice with those who rejoice, and weep with those who weep" (Rom. 12:15). Do you weep with those who weep?

Be Kind to One Another Paul says, "Be kind to one another" (Eph. 4:32). The Greek word translated "kind" means "serviceable, good, kind, gracious." The basic idea behind this word is "useful." A related form of this word is translated "kindness" in Galatians 5:22. Kindness is speaking kind words and doing acts of kindness.

A small act of kindness makes all the difference in the world for others and you. "Kindness makes a person attractive. If you would win the world, melt it, do not hammer it" (Alexander Maclaren). Somerset Maughan's mother was an extraordinarily beautiful woman married to an extraordinarily ugly man. When a family friend once asked how such a beautiful woman could have married such an ugly man, she replied, "He has never once hurt my feelings."

Summary: Because we are united to one another in Christ, we should lovingly relate to one another.

On June 9, 1985, Thomas Sutherland, an American who was dean of the American University's School of Agriculture in Beirut, was kidnapped by Islamic Jihad members near his Beirut home. He was held captive in Lebanon for six years and was finally released on November 18, 1991. After his release, he and his wife,

Jean, co-authored his memories of the experience (Thomas and Jean Sutherland, *At Your Own Risk*). During his captivity, he was put in isolation in a room without light. Three times, he thought of committing suicide but decided not to because of his wife and family. A pastor friend of mine telling the story concluded, "We all need relationships strong enough to keep us from quitting when circumstances get rough."

Charles Schulz's Philosophy

The following is the philosophy of Charles Schutz, the creator of the "Peanuts" comic strip.

1. Name the five wealthiest people in the world.
2. Name the last five Heisman trophy winners.
3. Name the last five winners of the Miss America pageant.
4. Name ten people who have won a Nobel or Pulitzer Prize.
5. Name the last half dozen Academy Award winners for best actor and actress.
6. Name the last decade's worth of World Series winners.

We do not remember yesterday's headliners. Even for the best achievers, the applause dies. Awards tarnish. Achievements are forgotten. Accolades and certificates are buried with their owners. Here's another quiz. See how you do on this one:

1. List a few teachers who aided your journey through school.
2. Name three friends who have helped you through a difficult time.
3. Name five people who have taught you something worthwhile.
4. Think of a few people who have made you feel appreciated and special.
5. Think of five people you enjoy spending time with.

The lesson: the people who make a difference in your life are not those with the most credentials, money, or awards. They are the ones who care.

Chapter 4

How To Serve At Church

We would all agree that we should relate to and get along with one another, especially at church. What would you say if I told you that just doing that is insufficient? The Lord expects more of believers, particularly at church.

The modern church has designated one or more individuals in a congregation as "ministers" and tagged the rest of the believers as "laymen." According to the Bible, all believers are in the ministry (Eph. 4:12). As a believer, you should be asking the question, "How can I minister to other believers?" Some phrases that include "one another" give us an insight into this issue.

Some of the commands in which that phrase is used inform us about how *not* to relate to one another (see the chapter entitled "How Not to Relate to One Another"). Some of the statements in which that phrase appears instruct us concerning how to relate to one another (see the chapter entitled "How to Relate to One Another"). Some examples in the latter category described how to relate to one another and how to *serve* one another. The Lord not only desires that we endeavor to keep the unity of the Spirit in the bond of peace and to relate to each other intimately; He wants us to serve one another.

Be a Benevolent Host

The Command Peter says, "But the end of all things is at hand; therefore be serious and watchful in your prayers. And above all things have fervent love for one another, for love will cover a multitude of sins. *Be* hospitable to one another without grumbling" (1 Pet. 4:7-9).

The Explanation Peter is teaching the end of everything we currently experience is the imminent coming of the Lord (1 Pet. 4:7a). To that, he adds a series of participles, all of which are grammatically dependent on the imperatives of 1 Peter 4:7. For example, be serious and watchful in prayer (1 Pet. 4:7b).

In verse 8, Peter begins a list of responsibilities that involve others. At the top of the list of responsibilities toward others is love (1 Pet. 4:8). Love for one another is to be fervent, a Greek word that means "stretched, strained." Because the end is pending, believers should actively and earnestly cultivate mutual love at its highest level.

A specific application of love is to "Be hospitable to one another without grumbling" (1 Pet. 4:9). The word hospitable means "lover of strangers." Thus, this command includes lodging believers from other places, but here, they are to show hospitality to believers within the local congregation. Perhaps opening one's home for church meetings is included (see the exercise of gifts mentioned in the following verses).

The Greek word "grumbling" means "murmuring, muttering." Its presence here seems to indicate that the demands for hospitality were frequent. Hospitality can be burdensome and costly. The temptation is to become irritated and resentful and to complain and murmur. The term "murmuring" refers to repeated expressions of complaints, often spoken to others with the result of stirring up rebellion. Believers are to practice hospitality with a loving heart and cheerful spirit, with graciousness, not grumbling, with pleasure, not displeasure.

Hospitality is using your home to house and feed others. In our day, it undoubtedly includes feeding others outside your house, such as taking a meal to a shut-in. There is a distinction between entertaining and hospitality. Entertaining people is showing off your house and your cooking abilities. Hospitality is opening your house to them. Entertaining centers on self and begs for compliments; hospitality centers on others and God.

John Piper says: "The physical force of gravity pulls everything to the center of the earth. In order to break free from earth-centered life, thousands and thousands of pounds of energy have to push the space shuttle away from the center. There is also a psychological force of gravity that constantly pulls our thoughts, affections, and physical actions inward toward the center of our own selves and our own homes. Therefore, the most natural thing in the world is to neglect hospitality. It is the path of least resistance. All we have to do is yield to the natural gravity of our self-centered life, and the result will be a life so full of self that there is no room for hospitality. We will forget about it. And we will neglect it. So the Bible bluntly says, Stop that! Build a launching pad. Fill up your boosters. And blast out of your self-oriented routine. Stop neglecting hospitality. Practice hospitality."

Hospitality does not have to be extravagant or fancy. It is sharing what you have. Karen Burton Mains, author of *Open Heart/Open Home*, writes, "One morning, I decided to read a novel instead of doing the housework. Of course, a person from church stopped by. The place was a mess—dishes in the sink, toys everywhere, last night's newspaper all over the floor." As she went to the door, she could hear her father's voice, "Hospitality comes before pride." Easy enough to say when your place is tidy. She swallowed her pride and let in the person from church. After they came in and sat down, her friend said, "I used to think you were perfect, but now I think we can be friends!" At the end of that chapter, she suggests that we should write down all the reasons we do not practice hospitality and put a "P" for pride beside each one.

Be a Burden Bearer

The Command Paul says, "Bear ye one another's burdens and so fulfill the law of Christ" (Gal. 6:2). In the immediate context, this verse is connected to Galatians 6:1 and means "bear the burden of the fall and failure of another. In so doing, you fulfill the law of Christ, which is love" (Jn. 13:34; Gal. 5:14; Jas. 2:18). The word "bear" means "to carry." It is used in the New Testament of carrying a water jar, a coffin, a stone, a corpse, a man, etc. The load may be heavy, but for love's sake, bear it. In light of the theme of the book, perhaps Paul is also saying, "If you must impose a burden on yourself, do not let it be the law. Rather, let it be the load of a weak, wounded brother."

A Clarification A few verses later, Paul adds, "For each one shall bear his own load" (Gal. 6:5). Each person is personally responsible. So examine yourself, prove yourself and rejoice in what God has done in your life. Don't lift yourself up by pulling someone else down (who is already down).

Paul wrote this letter to the Galatians to refute legalism. Legalists are not interested in bearing burdens. Instead, they add to the burdens of others (Acts 15:10). Jesus criticized the Pharisees for this sin. Concerning them, He said, "For they bind heavy burdens, hard to bear, and lay them on men's shoulders; but they themselves will not move them with one of their fingers" (Mt. 23:4). Believers are to bear the burdens of others. Paul presents the case of a believer who falls into sin. Nothing reveals the sin of legalism better than how legalists treat those who have sinned. In this paragraph, Paul contrasts how legalists and believers deal with someone caught in a sin. The legalists are more critical than they are caring! They are more of a hindrance than a help.

Some burdens are to be shouldered alone. A man in a supermarket was pushing a shopping cart that contained a screaming baby boy. As the man proceeded down the aisles, he kept saying, "Keep calm, George. Don't get excited, George. Don't yell, George." A lady watched with great admiration and finally spoke up and said, "You are certainly to be commended for your patience in trying to quiet little George." "Lady," he said, "I'm George!" Raising kids can be a real burden at times, and it is a burden that we have to bear by ourselves.

Some burdens are to be shed by casting them on the Lord (Ps. 55:22). Abraham Lincoln once said, "I have been driven many times to my knees by the overwhelming conviction that I had nowhere else to go." A boy and his dad were hiking together on a familiar path. As they made a sharp turn in a narrow section of the path, they came across a big rock blocking them. The little boy asked his father, "Do you think I can move it?" His dad said, "Why, of course, if you use all your strength. I'm sure you can move it." The little boy chose an angle of attack on the big rock and began pushing with everything he had. He grunted and groaned. Summoning all the strength he had, he pushed and pushed, but to no avail. Finally, in desperation, he said, "You were wrong, Dad. I can't do it." His dad looked him in the eyes, smiled, and said, "No, son, you haven't used all your strength yet. I'm right here and you haven't asked me to help you!"

Some burdens are to be shared with others. In his book, *Up from Slavery*, Booker T. Washington writes, "The most trying ordeal that I was forced to endure as a slave boy, however, was the wearing of a flax shirt. In the portion of Virginia where I lived, it was common to use flax as part of the clothing for the slaves. That part of the flax from which our clothing was made was largely the refuse, which, of course, was the cheapest and roughest part. I can scarcely imagine any torture, except, perhaps, the pulling of a tooth that is equal to that caused by putting on a new flax shirt for the first time. It is almost equal to the feeling that one would experience if he had a dozen or more chestnut burrs, or a hundred small pin-points, in contact with his flesh. Even to this day, I can recall accurately the tortures that I underwent when putting on one of these garments. The fact that my flesh was soft and tender added to the pain. But I had no choice. I had to wear the flax shirt or none, and had it been left to me to choose, I should have chosen to wear no covering. In connection with the flax shirt, my brother John, several years older than I am, performed one of the most generous acts I ever heard of one slave relative doing for another. On several occasions when I was being forced to wear a new flax shirt, he generously agreed to put it on in my stead and wear it for several days till it was 'broken in.' Until I had grown to be quite a youth, this single garment was all I wore."

A man fell into a pit and couldn't get himself out. An empathetic person said, "I feel for you down there." A Pharisee said, "Only bad people fall into pits." A gossip wanted to know all the details. A self-pitying person said, "You should see my pit." A fire-and-brimstone preacher said, "You deserve your pit." A psychologist noted, "Your parents are to blame for your pit." A self-esteem therapist said, "Believe in yourself and you can get out of the pit." An optimist said, "Things could be worse." A pessimist said, "There's nothing worse than this." Jesus, seeing the man, took him by the hand and lifted him out of the pit.

Lift a burden with a kind word, a note, a call, or tangible help because some burdens are meant to be shared.

Be a Builder of People

The Command Paul says, "Edify one another" (1 Thess. 5:11;

Rom. 14:19). The Greek verb translated "edify" means "to build a house, to build, to build up." It is used of rebuilding or restoring. It is translated "edify." The Greek noun means "building" and is used figuratively in the New Testament of "building up, edifying."

The Means One means of edification is love. Paul says, "Now concerning things offered to idols: We know we all have knowledge. Knowledge puffs up, but love edifies" (1 Cor. 8:1; see also 2 Cor. 10:8). In other words, knowledge puffs up; love builds up. Later, Paul says, "All things are lawful for me, but not all things are helpful; all things are lawful for me, but not all things edify" (1 Cor. 10:23).

Another means of edification is words. Paul also says, "Let no corrupt word proceed out of your mouth, but what is good for necessary edification, that it may impart grace to the hearers" (Eph. 4:29). The Greek word translated "corrupt" means "bad, worthless, rotten." Here, it is used figuratively for something "offensive and injurious." This injunction is not talking about lying. That has already been covered (Eph. 4:25).

The issue is edification. As pointed out, the Greek word "edification" means "to build up." What comes out of the believer's mouth should be good, not bad; wholesome, not worthless; redemptive, not rotten. The reason is "that it may impart grace to the hearers" (Eph. 4:29). The question is, "Does it build up or tear down? Does it inspire or injure?"

Those who have been recipients of grace (Eph. 1:6, 7; 2:5, 8) should minister grace.

Simon Cowell, one of the talent judges on the American Idol TV show, enjoyed tearing down the talentless. Here are some of his cutting comments: "If you lived 2,000 years ago and sang like that, they would have stoned you." "That was absolutely ghastly. I can honestly say if you won, it would be the end of the American music industry." "That was dreadful. Is singing something you want to pursue?" The contestant thought for a second and then said, "I can take it or leave it." With a sinister smile, Simon responded, "Leave it."

One of the finest ways to build people up is to let them know you believe in them. This faith cannot be patronizing. It must be sincere. A woman with great talent took a job below her abilities. Someone she worked with said, "What are you doing here?" The coworker encouraged her to develop her talent, which she went on to do. This is the type of thing that needs to be done spiritually. Tell believers you believe they can be spiritually mature.

A Builder or a Wrecker

As I watched them tear a building down.
A gang of men in a busy town
With a ho-heave-ho and a lusty yell
They swung a beam and the side wall fell
I asked the foreman, "Are these men skilled,
And the men you'd hire if you wanted to build?"
He gave a laugh and said, "No, indeed,
Just common labor is all I need."

"I can easily wreck in a day or two,
What builders have taken years to do."
And I thought to myself, as I went my way
Which of these roles have I tried to play?
Am I a builder who works with care,
Measuring life by rule and square?
Am I shaping my work to a well-made plan
Patiently doing the best I can?
Or am I a wrecker who walks to town
Content with the labor of tearing down?
"O Lord, let my life and my labors be
That which will build for eternity!"

Summary: Every believer is to minister to other believers by being a benevolent host, a burden bearer, and a builder of people.

In the 1950s, marketing whiz Stanley Arnold was working at Young & Rubicam, where he was asked to develop a marketing campaign for Remington Rand. The company was among the most conservative in America. At the time, its chairman was retired General Douglas MacArthur. Intimidated at first by a company that was so much a part of America, Arnold also found in that phrase the first inspiration for a campaign.

After thinking about it, he went to the New York offices of Merrill Lynch, Pierce, Fenner, and Beane and placed the ultimate odd-lot order: "I want to purchase," he told the broker, "one share of every single stock listed on the New York Stock Exchange." After a vice president tried to talk him out of it, the order was finally placed. It came to more than $42,000 for one share in each of the 1098 companies listed on the Big Board at the time. Arnold now took his diversified portfolio into a meeting of Remington Rand's board of directors, where he argued passionately for a sweepstakes campaign with the top prize, A Share in America.

The conservative old gentlemen shifted in their seats and discussed the idea for a while. "But Mr. Arnold," said one, "we are not in the securities business." Said another, "We are in the shaver business." "I agree that you are not in the securities business," said Arnold," but I think you also ought to realize that you are not in the shaver business either. You are in the people business." The company bought the idea (Peter Hay, *The Book of Business Anecdotes*, in *Bits and Pieces*, Oct. 1990).

Chapter 5

How To Minister At Church

According to the New Testament, the Pastor's job is to equip believers for their work of ministry (Eph. 4:12). Does that mean that the Pastor should teach people how to preach? Some will be relieved to learn the Scriptures do not expect you to preach, but that does not get you off the hook.

What, then, does your ministry look like? The expression "one another" tells us how to minister to one another as well as how to relate to one another. The overriding general principle for all relationships and ministry is love. We relate to one another by greeting one another, singing to one another, fellowshipping with one another, praying for one another, being compassionate toward one another, and being kind to one another. We serve one another by being a benevolent host, a burden bearer, and a builder of people. That is only the beginning. There is more, much more. Additional "one another" phrases tell us what we are to do to minister to one another.

For example, the book of Hebrews says, "Let us consider one another in order to stir up love and good works, not forsaking the assembling of ourselves together, as *is* the manner of some, but exhorting *one another,* and so much the more as you see the Day approaching" (Heb. 10:24-25). We are to *consider* one another so that we might *exhort* one another. Every believer is to be involved in the ministry of exhortation.

The Greek word rendered "exhorting" is pregnant with meaning. Consequently, it isn't easy to translate. Because it contains so many nuances, no English word can adequately translate it (see Barclay, *More New Testament Words*, p. 129). It means "calling to one's aid, summons," hence, "appeal, entreaty," and "exhortation, encouragement, consolation, comfort." It is used just over 100 times in the New Testament and is often translated "beseech" (Rom. 12:1; 15:30; 16:17; Eph. 4:1). Likewise, the Greek noun means "to call to one's aid" in a judicial sense, hence, "an advocate, pleader, intercessor." The noun is used of the Holy Spirit (Jn. 14:16; 14:26; 16:7) and Christ (1 Jn. 2:1). The basic concept of both the noun and the verb is "called alongside to help."

The verb is translated by three English words, each describing a ministry believers are to have to each other. Let's look at those three words plus one other word. These four words constitute a major part of every believer's ministry.

Comfort

The Command Paul says, "Comfort one another" (1 Thess. 4:18; 5:11). The Greek word translated "comfort" here is the same one rendered "exhorting" in Hebrews 10:25. Barclay says that in classical Greek, this verb means "to call in a counselor to give advice, to call in an advocate to plead a case in court and to call in the gods to help" (Barclay, pp. 130-131). In the Greek translation of the Old Testament, it means "one called into comfort and console" (Isa. 40:1-2; Barclay, p. 131).

There is another Greek word rendered "comfort." It also means "to encourage, exhort, comfort, console." It appears in John 11:19; 11:31; 1 Thessalonians 2:1; 5:14. The feminine noun form occurs in 1 Corinthians 14:3 and the masculine noun form occurs in Philippians 2:1. The former word is directed more toward the will, whereas this one is more toward the emotions.

The Explanation Paul went to Thessalonica, led people to Christ and told them the Lord was coming at any minute. Then, he left town. After his departure, some people in the congregation died. Those who survived were worried that those who had died would miss the rapture. Paul assures them that those who died would be raised first and we all together meet the Lord in the air (1 Thess. 4:15-17). He concludes by saying, "Comfort one another with these words." When people are sorrowing, comfort them.

The Application You can do this. It is your ministry. The question is, "How do you comfort someone?" Here are three principles of ministry and a specific suggestion for ministering to grieving people. These are simple things you need to do and you can do.

1. Be there. The most basic meaning of the Greek word "comfort" is "called alongside to help." Furthermore, the writer to the Hebrews speaks of "Not forsaking the assembling of ourselves together" (Heb. 10:25). If you are not present, you cannot minister to others. To minister, you need to be near the person. You need to

be there.

When I was in seminary, I became the pastor of a small rural church. I remember well the first time somebody in the church passed away and I, as the pastor, had to go see the family. I did not have a clue as to what to do. We had not covered house calls in the seminary yet, especially in a house full of bereaved people! I wondered, "What do you say?" I called an older, much more experienced pastor and asked, "What do I do now?" I particularly wanted to know what to say. I have never forgotten what he told me: "The most important thing you can do is just be there."

2. Listen. The writer to the Hebrews says, "Consider one another" (Heb. 10:24). The Greek word translated "consider" means "to take note of, perceive, consider carefully." While other things are, no doubt, involved, this includes listening. It has been said that 90% of the people who go to counselors do not want answers; they want someone to listen. When people are grieving the loss of a loved one, one of the ways to minister to them is to let them talk about that person. There may be exceptions to this rule; some may not want to talk. Considering one another includes being aware of where they are emotionally so you can be sensitive to what they need at the moment.

For ten years, I was on call for Forest Lawn Mortuary. If someone did not have a pastor, I was on the list of pastors called to conduct the funeral. Consequently, I have conducted hundreds of funerals. A family once requested that we invite people from the audience to tell what they remembered about the deceased person. It worked so well that I made it a standard practice to ask the family if they wanted to do that. Virtually all of them said, "Yes." In my opinion, the most effective ministry with bereaved people is to have them talk about the deceased person. That means we listen.

3. Identify with them. Part of the reason for considering one another is being able to relate to where they are. After you listen, you need to identify where they are so they will listen to you. The way to identify with people is to tell them about the same thing happening to you. If the same thing has not happened to you, tell them about something similar that has happened to you. If you cannot think of anything, repeat back to them what they have told you. They need to know you understand where they are.

In the first church I pastored, there was an elderly lady whose husband became terminally ill. After months of caring for him as well as their small business, he died. At that point, she was physically, mentally, emotionally, and spiritually spent. I went to see her to "comfort" her. At one point, she said to me, "Pastor, you don't know how I feel because you've never had a mate die." I thought to myself, "Lady, you are right." So, I went to see a woman in the community who had gone through the same thing. I went to see the second widow and asked her to visit the first lady. It worked because the two could identify with each other.

4. Give hope. In bereavement, a major issue is hope (1 Thess. 4:13). Notice Paul says, "Therefore comfort one another *with these words*" (1 Thess. 4:18). The words he has in mind are the words concerning the Lord's return and our gathering together with Him. Don't preach, but *after* you have identified with them,

when appropriate, comfort them with the Word, which is why you need to know the Word.

It is not just those who have lost someone in death who need comfort. It is anyone who has lost anything, including a job, their health, or maybe something much less serious. Losses cause sorrow and grief. You can comfort people going through such experiences by just being there, listening, identifying with them, and, depending on the situation, giving them a word of comfort from the Word.

The first step is to be there. Someone has written, "I can't give solutions to all of life's problems, but I can listen to you. I can't change your past with all its heartache and pain, nor the future with its untold stories, but I can be there now when you need me to care. Your joys, triumphs, successes, and happiness are not mine, yet I can share in your laughter. I can't keep your heart from breaking and hurting, but I can cry with you and help you pick up the pieces and put them back in place. I can't solve the problem, but I can love you and be your friend."

Exhort

The Command Paul says, "Exhort one another daily" (Heb. 3:13; 10:25). The Greek verb translated "exhort" in Hebrews 3:13 and Hebrews 10:25 is the same one translated "comfort" in 1 Thessalonians 4:18. Barclay says, in secular Greek, it means "to exhort or urge" (Barclay, p. 133). Plato exhorts men to apply their minds to think about things (*The Republic*, 535b). It was used to exhort troops about to go into battle (Barclay, p. 134).

The Explanation Hebrews was written to Jewish Christians contemplating forsaking Christianity and returning to Judaism. These people needed to be exhorted to go on to maturity (Heb. 6:1). When believers are slacking off, exhort them.

The Application The principles of ministry apply to those who need exhortation: be there, listen, and identify with them. Beyond that, in the case of exhortation, you need to urge them to continue toward the goal (Heb. 3:12-14). The essence of exhortation is urging people not to give up but to continue moving toward the goal. The adage says, "Give a man a good name and he will live up to it." Another way to exhort people is to remind them of the consequences (Heb. 3:15-17).

Again, the second principle of ministry is critical: listen. If you do not listen first, you will lose them. The following letter was left by a son who ran away from home. "Dear Folks, Thank you for everything, but I am going to Chicago to try and start a new life. You asked me why I gave you so much trouble, and the answer is easy for me to provide, but I wonder if you will understand.

"Remember when I was about six or seven and I used to want you to just listen to me? I remember all the nice things you gave me for Christmas and my birthday, and I was really happy with the things—for about a week—but the rest of the time I didn't really want presents. I just wanted you to listen to me like I was somebody who felt things too. But you said you were busy.

"Mum, you're a wonderful cook and have everything so clean. You were so tired from doing everything that made you busy, but you know something, Mum? I would have liked crackers and peanut butter just as much if you had only sat down with me during the day and said, ' Tell me all about it. Maybe I can help.'

"I think that all the kids who are doing so many things that grownups are tearing out their hair worrying about are really looking for somebody that will have time to listen a few minutes and who really will treat them as they would a grownup who might be helpful to them, you know.

"Anybody asks you where I am, tell them I've gone looking for somebody with time because I've got a lot of things I want to talk about. Love to all, your Son."

Encourage

The Concept No passage is translated "encourage one another," but Paul sent Timothy to "encourage" the church at Thessalonica (1 Thess. 3:2) and there is a gift of exhortation/encouragement (Rom. 12:8; see Acts 4:36). The Greek word translated "encourage" in 1 Thessalonians 3:2 is the same one that is translated "comfort" in 1 Thessalonians 4:18 and "exhort" in Hebrews 3:13 and Hebrews 10:25. Admittedly, there is an overlap between exhortation and encouragement.

Barclay says, "Again and again, we find that *parakalein* is the word of the rallying cry; it is the word used of the speeches of leaders and soldiers who urge each other on. It is the word used of words that would send fearful, timorous, and hesitant soldiers and sailors courageously into the battle. A *parakletos* is, therefore, an *encourager*, one who puts courage into the faint-hearted, one who nerves the feeble arm for fight, one who makes a very ordinary man cope gallantly with a perilous and a dangerous situation" (Barclay, p. 134).

The Explanation The believers in the church at Thessalonica were not slacking off, like the recipients of the book of Hebrews. The church was doing well spiritually (1 Thess. 1:3-8), yet Paul was concerned about their faith (1 Thess. 3:2, 5, 10) and their sanctification, especially their love (1 Thess. 4:3, 10). There was also a doctrinal question (1 Thess. 4:13-18) and there were difficulties in their meetings (1 Thess. 5:12, 19, 20). So, while they needed exhortation, as all of us do, what they needed was more like encouragement. Paul and Silas left Thessalonica when persecution broke out (Acts 17:1-10). Maybe the difference between exhorting and encouraging is the need for courage. They did not believe they could make it or do it. When believers are slipping, encourage them.

The Application Those who are facing challenging circumstances need courage. Larry Crabb, a Christian counselor, wrote a book entitled *Encouragement*. In it, he says, "*Encouragement is the kind of expression that helps someone want to be a better Christian, even when life is tough*" (Crabb, p. 10, italics his). He says that the theme of his book is "*encouragement through the careful selection of words that are intended to influence another person meaningfully toward increased godliness*" (Crabb, p. 20, italics his).

The principles of ministry apply to those who need encouragement: 1) be there (Paul did not just send a letter; he sent Timothy; 1 Thess. 3:2), 2) listen, and 3) identify with them. In the case of encouragement, the issue is faith (1 Thess. 3:2). They need to believe what God says. You can minister to them by letting them know you believe they can do whatever they need to do. That will give them the courage to do it. Someone has said, "The human spirit soars with hope when lifted by a word of encouragement."

In the opening paragraph of his book, Crabb states, "Encouragement is important business. It merits our careful attention, not only because Scripture tells us directly to think about it, but also because it represents the unique value of Christian fellowship. Any group of compatible people can enjoy themselves, but Christians can enrich their social enjoyment with the knowledge that when they spend time together, they can have an eternally significant impact on one another."

Crabb relates, "I can recall standing by the finish line at many track meets, waiting for my son to come straining down the last stretch of a two-mile run. Exhausted by the labor of pushing himself to his limit and sometimes bothered my variety of aches and cramps, he was sorely tempted to collapse 50 yards short of the finish line. As each of our team runners came into view, the line of paunchy, out-of-shape fathers would take up the cry, 'C'mon on, only a few yards to go! Push! Push! Kick up your legs! You can do it!' And most of the young athletes would respond to those words by grinning with determination, narrowing their eyes, and pumping their legs with renewed strength until they crossed the line. I have never yet heard a father call out to his son during that final stretch, 'You look tired! Why don't you quit? You are in the back third of the field anyway. Maybe running isn't your sport.' Yet I have overheard a Christian say to a young man after he had taught his first Sunday school class, "When is the regular teacher coming back?" There really isn't much difference between the words" (Crabb, p. 20).

Admonish

The Command Paul says, "Admonish one another" (Rom. 15:14). The Greek verb translated "admonish" is a compound word made up of the two Greek words "mind" and "to put or place," hence, it means "to put in mind, admonish, exhort." The noun is translated "admonition" (A-S). Trench, who wrote the classic work on Greek synonyms, says the distinctive feature of admonition is training with words and it frequently has the sense of admonishing with blame. He adds that it is training by a word of encouragement when sufficient but includes blame when required (Trench, pp. 112-114).

In its basic sense, blame is not necessarily present in admonition. For example, Paul says the Old Testament was written for our admonition (1 Cor. 10:11) and believers are to admonish one another in song (Col. 3:16; see also 1 Thess. 5:12; Eph. 6:4). On the other hand, the New Testament uses this word where blame is implied. For example, Paul exhorts believers to admonish the unruly (see 1 Thess. 5:14 where "warn" is the Greek word "admonish;" see also 2 Thess. 3:15; Titus 3:10). In the case of 1 Thessalonians 5:14, the idea of blame is embedded in the word "unruly." The Greek word translated "unruly" means "out of order, out of place." It was used of "soldiers not keeping rank and of an army in disarray" (A-S).

The Explanation In Romans, the issue was how they treated one another because of their disagreement over doubtful things.

The Application The principles of ministry apply to those who need admonition: 1) be there, 2) listen, and 3) identify with them. Beyond those principles, you need goodness, knowledge, and a brotherly manner. Paul says, "Now I myself am confident concerning you, my brethren, that you also are full of goodness, filled with all knowledge, able also to admonish one another" (Rom. 15:14) and "Yet do not count *him* as an enemy, but admonish *him* as a brother" (2 Thess. 3:15).

The Greek word translated "goodness" is moral goodness, which implies kindliness. In the context of Romans 15, "all knowledge" refers to their knowledge of amoral things. Paul is saying they had enough Christian character and spiritual maturity they would not injure the spiritual life of the weak by disregarding their conscience.

In the case of 1 Thessalonians 5:14, the one stepping out of line was the one who was refusing to work. The Greek word translated "unruly" is used of disorderly believers in 2 Thessalonians 3:11, where it is translated "disorderly." Paul says, "Yet do not count *him* as an enemy, but admonish *him* as a brother" (2 Thess. 3:15). As one commentator says, "While its tone is brotherly, it is big brotherly."

I was once the guest speaker in a church where this happened. A man in the church stopped working, ceased to support his family, and they had to go on welfare. Some of the men of the church "warned the unruly." They sat him down and said, "You need to go to work. Get a job." He did. Any time any believer steps out of line, believers around him should lovingly, yet firmly, admonish him to do what he knows he is supposed to do.

Summary: The way to minister to one another is to come alongside to help, comfort, exhort, encourage, and admonish one another by being there, listening, identifying, and speaking to the specific need as much as possible.

Some ministries are never said to be performed by "one another," such as teaching, reproving, rebuking, and restoring. For example, Paul says, "Brethren, if a man is overtaken in any trespass, you who *are* spiritual restore such a one in a spirit of gentleness, considering yourself lest you also be tempted" (Gal. 6:1). Those who are spiritually mature, not all believers, are to exercise the ministry of restoration.

The fact that the phrase "one another" is attached to each of these exhortations indicates that all believers are to perform all of these ministries. There are things you can do. (Be there. Listen. Identify.) Beyond the principles of ministry, when people are sorrowing, comfort them with hope. When slacking off, exhort them by pointing them toward the goal. When slipping, encourage them to keep the faith. When stepping out of line, admonish them by reminding them of their responsibility.

There are things you should *not* do, such as preach. Don't just say, "Don't worry, it will be OK," or "Just trust the Lord."

Someone has written, "One day, a teacher asked her students to list the names of the other students in the room on two sheets of paper, leaving a space between each name. Then she told them to think of the nicest thing they could say about each of their classmates and write it down. It took the remainder of the class period to finish their assignment, and as the students left the room, each one handed in the papers.

"That Saturday, the teacher wrote down each student's name on a separate sheet of paper and listed what everyone else had said about that individual. On Monday, she gave each student their list. Before long, the entire class was smiling. 'Really?' she heard whispered. "I never knew that I meant anything to anyone!" and "I didn't know others liked me so much" were most of the comments.

"No one ever mentioned those papers in class again. She never knew if they discussed them after class or with their parents, but it didn't matter. The exercise had accomplished its purpose. The students were happy with themselves and one another. That group of students moved on.

"Several years later, one of the students was killed in Vietnam and his teacher attended the funeral. She had never seen a serviceman in a military coffin before. He looked so handsome, so mature. The church was packed with his friends. One by one, those who loved him took a last walk by the coffin. The teacher was the last one to pass the coffin. One of the soldiers who acted as pallbearer approached her as she stood there. "Were you Mark's math teacher?" he asked. She nodded: "Yes." Then, he said, "Mark talked about you a lot."

"Most of Mark's former classmates attended a luncheon after the funeral. Mark's mother and father were there, obviously waiting to speak with his teacher. "We want to show you something," his father said, taking a wallet out of his pocket. "They found this on Mark when he was killed. We thought you might recognize it." Opening the billfold, he carefully removed two worn pieces of notebook paper that had been taped, folded, and refolded many times. The teacher knew without looking that the papers were the ones on which she had listed all the good things each of Mark's classmates had said about him. "Thank you so much for doing that," Mark's mother said. "As you can see, Mark treasured it."

"All of Mark's former classmates started to gather around. Charlie smiled rather sheepishly and said, "I still have my list. It's in the top drawer of my desk at home." Chuck's wife said, "Chuck asked me to put his in our wedding album."

"I have mine, too," Marilyn said. "It's in my diary." Then Vicki, another classmate, reached into her pocketbook, took out her wallet, and showed the group her worn and frazzled list. "I carry this with me at all times," Vicki said, and without batting an eyelash, she continued: "I think we all saved our lists."

"That's when the teacher finally sat down and cried. She cried for Mark and all his friends who would never see him again."

Words of love, comfort, encouragement, and exhortations are desperately needed and deeply appreciated. We need to minister to one another. We forget that life will end one day and don't know when that day will come. So, tell the people you love and care for that they are special and important. Tell them before it is too late.

Chapter 6

How To Be Christ-Like At Church

As we have seen, the Christian life in church involves several different things, including humbly seeking to maintain the unity of the Spirit in the bond of peace, relating to one another, serving one another, and ministering to one another. Underneath all of these activities is an attitude. What is that attitude?

Christ-Likeness

Christ One of Christ's characteristics was that He came to serve, not be served. "For even the Son of Man did not come to be served, but to serve, and to give His life a ransom for many" (Mk. 10:45). He served by teaching and healing. Serving is an activity, but it is also an attitude.

Us We are to be like Him. "For you, brethren, have been called to liberty; only do not *use* liberty as an opportunity for the flesh, but through love serve one another" (Gal. 5:13). The New Testament also speaks of "submitting to one another in the fear of God" (Eph. 5:21; 1 Pet. 5:5).

We can be either Christ-like or carnal. Paul told the Corinthians, "For you are still carnal. For where *there are* envy, strife, and divisions among you, are you not carnal and behaving like *mere men*?" (1 Cor. 3:3). Carnal believers live like ordinary humans, who are self-serving. Christ-like believers serve the Lord and others.

General William Booth founded the Salvation Army in the late nineteenth century. He was a remarkable man whose ministry has influenced countless numbers of people. Late in his life, General Booth could not attend one of the Salvation Army's international conventions because of his failing health. So he sent a telegram to the delegates at the convention bearing a message that contained one word: "OTHERS!"

Church is about people, not programs. By October 2005, the USC football team was a history-making powerhouse. They had won 27 games in a row, were ranked number one, and scored over 50 points per game in the 2005 season. At that point, a reporter interviewed the five defensive coordinators who had lost to the Trojans thus far in the season. The question was, "What game plan could stop this unstoppable force?" Bill Miller, the Arizona state's coordinator, who lost to USC 38 to 28, said, "It wasn't about the Xs and Os; it was about the Jimmys and Joes."

Not to Be Served

Some come to church to be served. Oh, they do not say that. They don't necessarily think that about themselves, but that is what is going on in their lives. They come with an attitude of, "I have arrived to serve you." Translated, that means, "I've arrived to be your savior." They come with an agenda.

1. Doctrine. Some come with a pet doctrine and are passionate about converting people to their point of view on that doctrine. There are two areas of doctrine people get emotionally hung up on and want to straighten everybody out about, namely, spiritual gifts and prophecy. Their attitude is, "I am here to straighten you and your church out. Your savior has arrived." Beware of Johnny-one-note.

2. Music. Some come with an ability to sing and they want to "serve" by singing. I once had a lady come to church—after the service. From the way she walked and the look in her eye, it was apparent she was on a mission. When she found me, she wasted no time getting to the point. She announced that she was leaving her church because they would not let her sing as much and she wanted to sing. She said all of the right "spiritual" things, such as, "God has given me a talent and I want to use it for His glory." When I informed her that our music program did not call for many solos, she turned on her heels, darted for the door, and I never saw her again.

Most are not that obvious; they are much more subtle, but they come with a hidden agenda. Their attitude is, "It's all about me."

3. Program. Some come with a program or project. Their attitude is, "My way is the right or better. Therefore, it is the only way."

4. Needs. Some come to get their needs met. This includes singles looking for a date or a mate. That one is not all bad, but meeting your needs should not be the primary reason for attending church.

Why do you go to church? Over the years, I have met people who attend church because of tradition, to please their wives, for status ("I attend the First Church"), or to feel good so they can make it through the next week. Watch out for Freddie-feel-good.

Then, some want to come and just sit. They have a balcony view of life. "I just want to watch." During football season, they take the couch potato view of life at home.

Oscar Wilde wrote what he called "the best short story in the world." W. B. Yeats quotes it in its original simplicity before it had been decorated and spoiled by the literary devices of its final form: "Christ came from a white plain to a purple city, and, as He passed through the first street, He heard voices overhead, and saw a young man lying drunk upon a window-sill. 'Why do you waste your soul in drunkenness?' He said. The man said, 'Lord, I was a leper, and you healed me; what else can I do?' A little farther through the town, He saw a young man following a harlot and said, 'Why do you dissolve your soul in debauchery?' And the young man answered, 'Lord, I was blind and You healed me; what else can I do?' At last, in the middle of the city, He saw an old man crouching, weeping on the ground, and, when he asked why he wept, the old man answered, 'Lord, I was dead, and you raised me into life; what else can I do but weep?'"

What else you can do is serve.

To Serve

Responsibility God has given believers *commands* to serve. These responsibilities include evangelism (Mk. 16:15), teaching (Col. 3:16), exhortation (Heb. 10:25), giving (1 Cor. 16:2), showing mercy (Jas. 2:12-13), etc. In one sense, to serve the Lord is to obey His commands.

As the story goes, during WW II, a group of French prisoners were forced to work in a German munitions factory. Upon realizing that the very bombs they were building were being used to destroy their beloved homeland, they began doing things that would create a malfunction in the devices that detonated the bombs. The bombs were designed to explode on impact. But with the changes, the prisoners made the bombs were harmless and when they hit, they did not explode. Puzzled by so many failed attacks, the French government conducted an investigation. Upon opening the bombs, they found slips of paper inside with the words: "We are doing the best we can with what we've got, where we are, every chance we get." That ought to be the attitude of every believer.

Special Ability God has also given each believer at least one *spiritual gift* (1 Cor. 12:7; Eph 4:7). A spiritual gift is a divinely given (Rom. 12:6; Eph. 4:7; 1 Cor. 12:7; 1 Pet. 4:10) ability to serve (1 Pet. 4:10). Four passages in the New Testament list 18 spiritual gifts (Rom. 12:6-8; 1 Cor. 12:10-12; 12:28-30; Eph. 4:11).

These 18 gifts can be divided into categories. Peter divides gifts into two categories: speaking gifts and serving gifts (1 Pet. 4:10-11). There is a third classification of gifts. Mark 16:15-20 mentions *signs* that would confirm the message of the gospel. Hebrews 2:2-3 speaks of confirming the message by *gifts* of the

Holy Spirit. Therefore, there are three types of gifts: speaking gifts, serving gifts (1 Pet. 4:7-11), and sign gifts (Mk. 16:15-20; Heb. 2:2-3).

The sign gifts include miracles (see taking up serpents and drinking deadly poison in Mk. 16:18), healings (see laying hands on the sick in Mk. 16:18 and casting out demons in Mk. 16:17), tongues (Mk. 16:17), and interpretation of tongues (the interpretation of tongues goes with tongues).

There is evidence that the sign gifts have ceased. In Ephesians, Paul says that the gifts of apostle and prophet are the foundation (Eph. 2:20, 3:5). Virtually all agree that there are no apostles now, which suggests that some of the gifts have ceased. In 1 Corinthians, Paul says, "Truly the signs of an apostle were accomplished among you with all perseverance, in signs and wonders and mighty deeds" (2 Cor. 12:12). Does not this imply that the sign gifts were unique to the Apostles and not by other believers? They would not have been signs of an apostle if everyone did them.

The gifts that have ceased are apostle, prophet, discernment, miracles, healing, tongues, and the interpretation of tongues. That leaves eleven gifts: the speaking gifts (evangelism, teaching, word of knowledge, word of wisdom, pastor/teacher, exhortation) and the serving gifts (administration, faith, giving, helps, showing mercy).

Now, notice that every believer is responsible for evangelizing, yet some are given the gift of evangelism. All are given the responsibility to teach and some are gifted at it. Every believer is to give, show mercy, etc.; some are gifted in these areas. In other words, God has given *responsibility* to all and *special ability* to some.

What is your attitude when you come to church?

When we come to church, we do not use the gifts we have. A young fellow was trying to express his love for his girlfriend. "Honey, I wish I was an octopus. Then I would have eight arms to hug you." The girl replied, "You know you are not telling the truth, for you are not using the two arms you have." Many believers are not using what the Lord has given them.

When we come to church, we do nothing. In his book *Keeping Pace*, Ernest Fitzgerald tells the story of a wealthy English philanthropist named Jeremy Bentham. In his will, Mr. Bentham bequeathed a fortune to a London hospital on whose Board of Directors he had sat for years. There was one peculiar stipulation. Mr. Bentham's will said that for the hospital to keep the money, Jeremy Bentham had to be present at every board meeting. So, for over 100 years, the remains of Jeremy Bentham were brought to the board room every month and placed at the head of the table. For over 100 years, in the secretary's minutes were the words, "Mr. Jeremy Bentham, present but not voting." Many Christians are present but not working. They are on the side-line, not the front-lines.

When we come to church, we want someone else to serve. A mother was preparing pancakes for her sons, Kevin, age 5 and Ryan, age 3. The boys began to argue over who would get the first pancake. Their mother saw the opportunity for a moral lesson. "If Jesus were sitting here, He would say, 'Let my brother have the first pancake, I can wait.'" Kevin turned to his younger brother and said, "Ryan, you be Jesus!"

Summary: The way to be Christ-like at church is to come with an attitude to serve, not to be served.

Larry Crabb wrote a book on marriage entitled *The Marriage Builder*. In it, he says that married people either practice ministry or manipulation. It seems to me that people come to church with either an attitude of ministering to others or manipulating others to get their needs met.

Writer Leo Rosten said, "I cannot believe that the purpose of life is to be happy. I think the purpose of life is to be useful, to be responsible, to be compassionate. It is, above all, to matter: to count, to stand for something, to have made some difference that you lived at all."

Objection: if I meet the needs of others, who meets my needs? In the comic strip Peanuts, Lucy asks Charlie Brown, "Why are we here on earth?" Charlie Brown replies, "To make others happy." Lucy ponders his reply for a moment and then asks, "Then why are the others here?"

I have three responses to that cartoon. 1) That kind of selfish thinking prevents you from thinking of others. 2) Maybe if you thought about others, others would think about you. 3) Perhaps that is when you get to know the Lord at a much deeper level.

Church is about serving, not being served. In 1973, Dr. Vernon Grounds, then president of Denver Seminary, challenged the graduating class with the truth of John 13, where the account of

Jesus washing the disciples' feet is found. Dr. Grounds told the graduates he would present a tangible symbol that could help them in their future ministries. As the classmates filed quietly to the front, they wondered what it would be—a special Scripture verse, a little book, an inscribed medallion. To their surprise, it was a small square of white terrycloth. One graduate, who has served as an overseas missionary, said, "We were commissioned to go into the world as servants. That small towel, frayed and grubby from years in my wallet, is a constant reminder of that moving moment and our basic call to serve."

Chapter 7

How To Be A Christian Boss

We spend a considerable portion of life at work. If you work eight hours per day, and many work more than that, you spend a third of the workweek at work. If you work 40 hours a week from the time you are 18 years old until you are 65, you will work 94,000 hours in your lifetime (47 years x 50 weeks x 40 hours = 94,000). Among other things, that means that if you are going to live a Christian life, you have to figure out how to do it at work.

You are either a "boss" or you are an employee. You are either over people or you are under a foreman, a supervisor, or a manager. God has something to say to both employers and employees. This chapter will consider what he says to the "boss," and the next will examine what He says to the employee.

This applies to anyone who is "over" others. That includes parents, teachers, policemen, and clerks dealing with customers. In the final analysis, God's words to the "boss" apply to all relationships.

The Institution of Slavery

Two passages in the New Testament instruct masters on how to treat slaves. Paul wrote both of them. He says, "And you, masters, do the same things to them, giving up threatening, knowing that your own Master also is in heaven, and there is no partiality with Him" (Eph. 6:9) and "Masters, give your bondservants what is just and fair, knowing that you also have a Master in heaven" (Col. 4:1). The New Testament seems to accept slavery as a fact of life. It does not call for the abolition of slavery. Several issues need to be considered.

The Political Issue One estimate is that there were 60,000,000 slaves in the Roman Empire. That means that there were two or three times more slaves than freemen. The sudden abolition of slavery would have caused chaos. Neither free men nor slaves were prepared for such a radical change. People needed to be educated before such radical reform could take place.

The Social Issue It is hard for us to imagine, but slavery played a useful social role in Roman society. It many cases, it benefited the slave. "It was more merciful to enslave a prisoner than to sacrifice him to the gods, to torture him to death, or to eat him. And the enslaved prisoner and the warrior who captured him at once became mutually useful to another. The warrior protected his slave from attack, and the slave, by his labor, left the warrior to protect him. Thus, each did something for the benefit of the other and the society in which they lived" (Plummer, *The Pastoral Epistles*, p. 177).

Jesus told a parable about a landowner and hired laborers (Mt. 20:1-16). Commenting on that story, Barclay says that the hired laborers were not slaves. They were hired laborers, the lowest class of workers. Slaves were more fortunate than hired laborers because, to some extent, they were regarded as being attached to the family and, therefore, were never in any imminent danger of starvation. On the other hand, day-laborers were entirely at the mercy of chance employment, always living on the edge of semi-starvation. If they were unemployed for one day, their family would go hungry (Barclay).

The Spiritual Issue What the New Testament teaches gradually reformed slavery. The church taught that slaves were to be treated as equals. Clement of Alexandria pleaded that "slaves are like ourselves" and that the golden rule applied to them. Lactantius wrote: "Slaves are not slaves to us. We deem them brothers after the Spirit, in religion fellow-servants." "Although there were thousands of slaves in the Christian Church, the inscription *slave* is never met with in the Roman Christian tombs. It was possible for a slave to hold high office in the Christian Church. In the early second century, two bishops of Rome, Callistus and Pius, had been slaves. And it was not uncommon for elders and deacons to be slaves" (Barclay on Matthew, vol. I, p. 388).

Hodge says, "The result of such obedience, if it could become general, would be, at first, the evils of slavery, and then slavery itself, would pass away as naturally and as healthfully as children cease to be minors." (For analysis and application of this concept to today's situation, see Plummer, pp. 185-187.)

In his book, *The Decline and Fall of the Roman Empire*, Edward Gibbon says, "While that great body [the Roman Empire] was invaded by open violence or undermined by slow decay, a pure and humble religion gently insinuated itself into the minds of men, grew up in silence and obscurity, derived new vigor from opposition, and finally erected the triumphant banner of the cross on the ruins of the capital." Christianity is more than a conqueror through Him who loves us.

The Instructions to Masters

Know You Have a Master Both passages about masters inform them that they have a Master in heaven ("knowing that your own Master also is in heaven" in Eph. 6:9 and "knowing that you also have a Master in heaven" in Col. 4:1).

In today's working environment, a boss, even a business owner, has bosses. Federal laws, state laws, local laws, company policies, and professional ethics must be obeyed. Beyond those layers of regulations, Christian masters have a Master in heaven. The heavenly Master will one day judge human masters. Christian masters are spiritual slaves to Christ.

Do Not Threaten (Eph. 6:9b). In the Roman world, slave owners had absolute rights over their slaves. Slaves were viewed as being only animated tools. The master could scourge and even kill his slaves. Slaves did not have the right to marry. If they did cohabitate and there was a child, the child belonged to the master "as the lamb of the flock belong to the shepherd" (Barclay on Col. 4:1). Moreover, being looked upon as "scarcely human," slaves lost all self-respect.

Since masters had absolute authority over their slaves, it was easy for them to mistreat them. Plato said, "The treatment of slaves is a test of character because a man could so easily wrong them with impunity" (cited by Eadie on Eph. 6). Unjust and cruel punishments were familiar features of slavery. Threatening was prevalent. Slaves were "kept in line" by intimidating looks, promises of severe punishment and the ever-present sight of the scourge (Eadie).

Paul admonishes slave owners not to threaten slaves. "The threatening tone must be heard no more" (Robinson). They must not adopt a "browbeating attitude" (Bruce). Peter says that when Christ suffered, He did not threaten (1 Pet. 2:23). Christian masters are to be Christ-like, giving up threats. Even the Old Testament gives this counsel: "You shall not rule over him with rigor, but you shall fear God" (Lev. 25:43).

The reason for giving up threatening is "knowing that your Master also is in heaven and there is no partiality with Him" (Eph. 6:9c). Masters have a Master in heaven to whom they are responsible for treating those under them. The issue is not what the civil law allows but what the law of love allows (Hodge).

There is a difference between warning and threatening. A warning assumes there is a company policy that has been violated. In such a case, it is the boss's responsibility to caution the employee concerning the consequences of another violation in the future. Warnings are perfectly proper. A threat is a personal decision designed to frighten.

A warning *informs*. A threat *intimidates*. A warning notifies a person, "You are harming yourself." A threat bullies someone with statements such as, "I can make life very difficult for you."

In a company that employed many salesmen, one manager motivated them by threats and intimidation. If a salesman was not selling, the manager would call him into his office and, with a sober expression on his face, tell him to put his keys and briefcase on the desk. He would inform him that he was fired. If the salesman asked why he was being fired, the manager would tell him it was because of a lack of production, but if he wanted to keep his job, he had to meet certain criteria. Those criteria included making five appointments daily by making 40 phone calls daily. The man who related the story to me said, "It never worked."

Just In 1887, in a letter to Bishop Mandell Creighton, Lord Acton wrote, "Power tends to corrupt, and absolute power corrupts absolutely. Great men are almost always bad men." Paul tells slave owners to do what is just, that is, what is right and correct. Because of the righteous character of God, treating people justly is morally right, even when it is not legally necessary.

Companies and bosses violate this concept every day. Over the years, I have heard many stories of bosses treating people unjustly. Typical are the cases of bosses telling the employee to do something unethical or illegal. In one such case, a company entered into an agreement with a broker who was to be paid for bringing deals to the company. The agreement included a list of people who were excluded. In other words, if the broker brought people on that list to the table, he would not be paid because the company already had contact with those individuals. The broker brought a deal to the company with the name of a man whose name sounded like someone on the exclusion list. The boss of the company told an employee to tell the broker they would not pay him for that deal because the person was on the exclusion list. That was simply not true. That was the unjust treatment of the employees as well as the broker.

On the other hand, some companies and bosses are just. In one situation, an employee had a quota. His boss said, "I am aware that things beyond your control affect your production. When I evaluate your production, I will consider those factors."

Fair The idea is that masters are to render evenhanded, impartial treatment. The master is still the master, but Christianity has regulated all his transactions with those under him. The motivation is that human masters need to know that they have a divine master in heaven. Masters have a master who is no respecter of persons. So, they should not show respect of persons either. Today, this is called discrimination.

Companies and bosses violate this concept every day. They pay one person a lower wage than another for the same job. I heard of a fellow who was given a sizable amount of stock options. The only caveat was that he had to work for 20 years to be vested. That was the company policy to keep good employees from leaving the company. Bob was a good employee for 19 years. Before he could make it to his 20th year, they fired him so they would not have to give him the stock options. That is not right, but when that happens to Bob and not everybody else, it's not fair. He sued and won a half-million dollars.

Summary: The way for Christian bosses to live the Christian life at work is to remember that they have a Master in heaven, so they do not threaten but treat the people under them justly and fairly.

There are practical reasons why these concepts should be implemented at work. Companies ought to be concerned about this because it affects their company. I have been told that the number one reason people leave their jobs is their boss.

Bosses ought to be concerned. United Airlines' Shuttle by United commissioned a survey that Louis Harris and Associates conducted. They surveyed 1000 business travelers. They discovered that "given the choice, most business travelers would rather sit next to a co-worker than the boss on flights as long as their colleagues do not talk too much. Of business travelers expressing a preference, 58% said they would not mind sitting next to the boss, but 87% preferred a fellow employee as a seatmate. Younger travelers want to be farthest from the boss. 54% of travelers between 18 and 29 strongly favored a seat far from the boss. Would the employees who work for you want to sit next to you? They would likely want to sit next to a just and fair boss who did not intimidate them.

Believers must be concerned about how bosses treat the people under them because they are answerable to the Lord.

A commentator, writing in 1810 when there were slaves in this country, said, "And with respect to all servants of every denomination, *equity* requires that we treat them with humanity and kindness: that we endeavor to make their service easy and their condition comfortable; that we forbear harsh and passionate language; that we overlook accidental errors, and remit trivial faults; that we impose only such labor as is reasonable in itself and suitable to their captivity; that our reproofs be calm and our counsels well timed; that the restraints we lay upon them be prudent and salutary; that we allow them reasonable time for rest and refreshment, for the culture of their minds, and for attendance on the worship of God; that we set before them a virtuous example, instill in them useful principles, warn them against wickedness of every kind, especially against sin which most easily besets them; that we offer them opportunity for reading and private devotion, and furnish them with the necessary means of learning the way of salvation; that we attend to the preservation of their health, and have compassion on them in sickness; and in a word that we contribute all possible assistance to render them useful, virtuous and happy" (Lathrop quoted by Eadie).

Chapter 7

How To Be A Christian Employee

We love to hate work. Someone has put it like this: "In prison, you spend most of your time in an 8 x 10 cell. You spend most of your time at work in a 6 x 8 cubicle. In prison, you get three meals a day. You only get a break for one meal at work and pay for it. In prison, you get time off for good behavior. At work, you get more work for good behavior. In prison, the guard locks and unlocks all the doors for you. You must carry a security card at work and open all the doors for yourself. In prison, you can watch TV and play games. At work, you get fired for watching TV and playing games. In prison, they allow your family and friends to visit. At work, you can't even speak to your family. In prison, the taxpayers pay all expenses with no work required. You get to pay all the expenses to go to work, and the government deducts taxes from your salary to pay for prisoners. In prison, you spend most of your life inside bars, wanting to get out. You spend most of your time at work wanting to get out and go inside bars. In prison, you must deal with sadistic wardens. At work, they are called managers."

What does God say about our work? How can we be Christian employees? In the epistles, five passages address this issue (Eph. 6:5-8; Col. 3:22-15; 1 Tim. 6:1-2; Titus 2:9-10; 1 Pet. 2:18). These passages overlap each other, but each contributes to an overall picture of how to be a Christian employee. Four of the five are addressed to slaves. As was mentioned in the previous chapter, the New Testament does not advocate the abolition of slavery, but its principles ultimately resulted in just that. The spiritual principles given to slaves in the first century apply to employees today.

Reverently Obey

Two of the five passages are virtually identical. In Ephesians, Paul wrote, "Bondservants, be obedient to those who are your masters according to the flesh, with fear and trembling, in sincerity of heart, as to Christ, not with eye service, as men-pleasers, but as bondservants of Christ, doing the will of God from the heart, with goodwill doing service, as to the Lord, and not to men, knowing that whatever good anyone does, he will receive the same from the Lord, whether *he is* a slave or free" (Eph. 6:5-8). To the Colossians, Paul said, "Bondservants, obey in all things your masters according to the flesh, not with eyeservice, as men-pleasers, but in sincerity of heart, fearing God. And whatever you do, do it heartily, as to the Lord and not to men, knowing that from the Lord, you will receive the reward of the inheritance; for you serve the Lord Christ. But he who does wrong will be repaid for what he has done, and there is no partiality" (Col 3:22-25).

In these passages, Paul issues one basic command and piles one phrase upon another to clarify it. The command is simple enough. It is "be obedient," but that command needs clarification. For example, throughout these passages, Paul repeatedly emphasizes to whom the obedience is to be rendered. It is to be rendered to "your master according to the flesh" (Eph. 6:5; Col. 3:22), but the phrase "according to the flesh" suggests an employee has two masters, one heavenly and one earthly.

The Human Boss While believers are to obey their human boss, they are to do it "not with eye service, as men-pleasers" (Eph. 6:6; Col. 3:22), "not to men" (Eph 6:7; Col. 3:23).

Eye service is a service that the human eye can see. The people performing this kind of work perform only when they are being watched and only enough to satisfy the minimum standards of their master. Slaves usually work with the motive of not being punished. Consequently, they only worked to please the master when he was watching; they would trifle in his absence. Do not be a "man-pleaser" or a "clock watcher" (Bruce).

In the final analysis, it is impossible to please people. An old fable passed down for generations tells about an older man traveling with a boy and a donkey. As they walked through a village, the man led the donkey, and the boy walked behind. The townspeople said the old man was a fool for not riding, so he climbed up on the animal's back to please them. When they came to the next village, the people said the old man was cruel in letting the child walk while he enjoyed the ride. So, to please them, he got off, set the boy on the animal's back, and continued. In the third village, people accused the child of being lazy for making the old man walk, and the suggestion was made that they both ride. Therefore, the man climbed on, and they set off again. In the fourth village, the townspeople were indignant at the cruelty to the donkey because he had to carry two people. The frustrated man was last seen carrying the donkey down the road.

The Divine Boss Believers are to obey "as to Christ" (Eph. 6:5; Col. 3:23), "as bondservants of Christ, doing the will of God from the heart" (Eph. 6:6; "And whatever you do, do it heartily, as to the Lord" in Col. 3:23) and "as to the Lord" (Eph 6:7). The ultimate boss is the Lord.

This obedience is not a begrudging obedience or a mechanical obedience. It is a hearty, eager obedience. In that it is unto the Lord, it is a reverent obedience. Paul says believers are to obey "with fear and trembling, in sincerity of heart, as to Christ" (Eph. 6:5). The fear and trembling is toward God (Col. 3:23). Believers are to sincerely regard their obedience to their masters as obedience to Christ. It is "goodwill doing service, as unto the Lord" (Eph. 6:7). Simply put, "And whatever you do, do it heartily, as to the Lord and not to men" (Col. 3:23). That is reverent obedience.

The reason such service is to be rendered is "that whatever good anyone does, he will receive the same from the Lord" (Eph. 6:8; Col. 3:24-25). At the judgment seat of Christ, servants will be rewarded for work they did for their human master, provided it was done as unto the Lord.

In ancient times, a sculptor was employed to construct a statue to stand in a Greek temple. He meticulously and conscientiously made a beautiful and ornate statue, even the part against the wall. When asked why he carved the back with the same care as the front, he replied, "That's the way I always work. Men may never see it, but I believe the gods do." He, of course, was mistaken about the gods, but the Christian slave who works with the same attitude about God is not.

In his autobiography, *A Life in Our Times*, John Kenneth Galbraith illustrates the devotion of Emily Gloria Wilson, his family's housekeeper. "It had been a wearying day, and I asked Emily to hold all telephone calls while I had a nap. Shortly thereafter, the phone rang. Lyndon Johnson was calling from the White House. 'Get me Ken Galbraith. This is Lyndon Johnson.' 'He is sleeping, Mr. President. He said not to disturb him.' 'Well, wake him up. I want to talk to him.' 'No, Mr. President. I work for him, not you.' When I called the President back, he could scarcely control his pleasure. 'Tell that woman I want her here in the White House'" (*Reader's Digest*, December 1981).

Respectfully Serve

Honor Unbelievers "Let as many bondservants as are under the yoke count their own masters worthy of all honor so that the name of God and *His* doctrine may not be blasphemed. And those who have believing masters, let them not despise *them* because they are brethren, but rather serve *them* because those who are benefited are believers and beloved. Teach and exhort these things" (1 Tim 6:1-2). As is evident from the phrase "And those who have believing masters" (1 Tim. 6:2), this passage speaks to slaves who have unbelieving masters (1 Tim. 6:1) and to those who have believing masters (1 Tim. 6:2).

Christian slaves are to give "all" honor, even to unbelieving masters. Slaves are to honor their masters because of their position. Slaves are to have an inner attitude of genuine respect for their masters.

The expression "under the yoke" highlights the "oppressive character" of the institution of slavery. The Greek word translated "masters" means "master, lord." It is the Greek word from which we get the English word "despot."

Peter echoes this when he says, "Servants, *be* submissive to *your* masters with all fear, not only to the good and gentle but also to the harsh" (1 Pet 2:18). The Greek word translated "servants" is not the usual word for servant in the New Testament, nor is it the word for slave. The Greek word for servant here denotes a household servant, a domestic, including freemen as well as slaves. The servants and slaves employed in the house were more exposed to the vicious temper and vices of the master than those in the field. It was "one of the most demeaning and difficult of all working relationships" (Adams).

Submission with the right attitude is to be rendered to all masters regardless of their treatment of the servant. Some bosses are good and gentle. They are kind and benevolent. The Greek word translated "gentle" includes the concepts of being considerate, fair, and reasonable (Stibbs/Walls). Others are "harsh," a Greek word that means "crooked, bent." It is the opposite of straight.

It describes crooked, perverse, unjust treatment. Such people are unkind, unfair, unreasonable, and unjust. They have been said to be "dishonest" and "morally evil," which suggests "not only physical mistreatment but also dishonesty regarding pay, working conditions, expectations, etc." (Grudem).

When treated harshly, people tend to complain, be insubordinate, hate the perpetrator, and want to get even. The modern American response is to demand our rights and sue. According to Peter, regardless of the treatment received, the servant is to be submissive with a "respectful attitude" toward God. Bad treatment is no excuse for a bad attitude or bad behavior.

The reason for honoring unbelieving masters is "so that the name of God and *His* doctrine may not be blasphemed" (1 Tim. 6:1b). In honoring their masters, slaves are honoring God. The Greek word translated "blaspheme" means "to speak lightly or profanely of sacred things, to blaspheme, especially God, to revile, rail at, slander." The behavior of believers can cause the name of God or the teaching of God (Guthrie says "the Christian faith") to be blasphemed.

I once worked for an *unbelieving* boss who did things I did not respect. For one thing, he lied to people. It was easier for him to lie than tell the truth. He also cheated people out of money, including me. As long as I did not have to lie and cheat, it was my Christian duty to honor his position, even when I did not respect his personal behavior.

Do Not Despise Believers "And those who have believing masters let them not despise *them* because they are brethren"

(1 Tim. 6:2a). Slaves who had believing masters had an added element to their situation, namely, that their masters were fellow believers. As believers, these slaves experienced spiritual freedom and, no doubt, enjoyed being treated as equals in the assembly of believers (Gal. 3:28). They enjoyed equality in the church and inferiority in their household (Guthrie). They had spiritual freedom and social bondage (Gromacki). Given that situation, slaves might think that their boss should give them their freedom.

The Greek word translated "despise" means "to think little of, despise." It is a compound word made up of the two words "think" and "down." Believing slaves are not to "think down" (Gromacki) or "look down" (Kent) on believing masters. They are not to "disdain" their masters (Hiebert). They are spiritual equals with their masters, but they are not "to pour mental contempt" on their owners for failure to release them. Slaves probably reasoned that since both they and their owners were delivered from bondage to sin, the owners should follow Christ's example and free their slaves.

The reason slaves are not to despise their masters is that they are brothers. Brothers are not to despise brothers. In other words, being believers, slaves should change their perception of their relationship with their masters. Instead of thinking of their masters as owners/masters, they should think of them as brothers. Of course, the master/slave relationship was still binding. The Lord did not change that (1 Cor. 7:20-24). Nevertheless, believing slaves were to respond to their believing masters as brothers.

Serve Them "But rather serve *them* because those who are benefited are believers and beloved" (1 Tim. 6:2b). Rather than despise their masters, slaves are to serve their believing masters. Actually, slaves were obligated to do that anyway, but now they were to render "exceptional service" (Hendriksen). The Greek word translated "rather" means "very, very much, exceedingly, more, rather." Kent says that here, it means "more." The fact that their masters are fellow believers should inspire them to faithful service because their service now benefits a beloved fellow believer.

I once had a *believing* boss who made decisions I did not respect. They were not unethical decisions; they were unwise. His decision and his treatment of others affected my attitude. I learn not to despise him but to serve him.

Resist Temptation

"Exhort bondservants to be obedient to their own masters, to be well-pleasing in all *things,* not answering back, not pilfering, but showing all good fidelity, that they may adorn the doctrine of God our Savior in all things" (Titus 2:9-10). These verses overlap what Paul has said in other passages. They also contain several ideas that have not been discussed previously.

Be Submissive For one thing, the Greek word translated "obedient" is not the normal Greek word for obey; it is stronger (Guthrie)! It includes obedience, but it is more than that. It means "to be in subjection." Furthermore, it is in the middle voice, indicating that it is something you do, not something done to you or forced upon you. In other words, Paul says, "voluntarily submit to your master." What he is demanding is an attitude of a submissive spirit.

Have a Pleasing Spirit Paul says, "to be well-pleasing in all things." There must be an internal attitude of wanting to please the master. The problem is that Paul says, "in all things." Is this to be taken absolutely? Suppose the master demanded that the slave lie, steal, or murder. Must he please him, then? The answer, of course, is "No." The purpose clause at the end of verse 10 implies a limitation. By sinning, the slave would not be adorning the doctrine of God (Hendriksen).

The positive side is "but showing all good fidelity" (Titus 2:10). A laborer is to be faithful and trustworthy (Hiebert). You owe your boss your loyalty. If you have to choose between your boss and your buddies, you should be loyal to your boss.

Suppose your boss is asking you to do something illegal or immoral. Is there a limit to loyalty? The answer is "Yes," for Paul says, "all *good* fidelity." This loyalty does not extend to crime and wrongdoing. It is to be exercised in everything good and beneficial (Hiebert).

Answering Back "Answering back" is a weak translation. Paul says, "Don't contradict, oppose, resist." Paul is not talking about talking, which is contrary; he refers to setting oneself against another's plans, wishes, and orders (Ellicott). This word has overtones of resistance and rebellion (Hendriksen; Rom. 10:21; Heb. 12:3; Jude 11).

How To Be A Christian Employee

One worker said, "I worked in a factory of over 400 people. I'd say that 70% of them did not like what they were doing; many spent more time trying to get out of work than doing it. Instead of trying to do something with themselves to find a better job, people just complained." We gossip ("Did you hear about so and so?"). We complain ("Did you know Joe got a raise?"). We murmur ("I can't stand my boss. I hate this company.).

Pilfering The Greek word translated "pilfering" was the usual Greek word for petty theft. Pilfering was a common vice of slaves. Christian slaves, like non-Christian slaves, were no doubt tempted to rationalize, "The master owes me this and more. He has taken away my freedom and robbed me of my strength and talent without adequate compensation" (Hendriksen).

Pilfering is a major social problem today. Employees pilfer time, materials, and money. Crime committed by the workforce has been called the biggest business in America today. It costs United States companies billions of dollars a year, more than street robberies and burglary losses combined. According to security experts, as many as 70% of employees occasionally steal, about half of which is petty pilfery: the garage mechanic who pockets a sparkplug, the typist who lifts a box of paperclips, the mailroom clerk who slips some personal letters through the meter machine, the executive who pads his expense account, the meatpacker who goes home with a steak tucked in a folded newspaper, the office worker who makes personal long-distance phone calls. This type of mini-theft might seem like nothing more than a worker who sneaks a fistful of toothpicks out of a lumber mill, but it packs a big wallop because the practice is so widespread. In the retail industry, internal thievery outstrips shoplifting.

When I was in seminary, I had a job at a factory. One morning, I arrived at work and discovered that the men in my department were working on a project I didn't recognize. When I asked the foreman about the new job, he told me it was government work. That surprised me because that factory didn't have any government contracts. When I asked him what he meant, he informed me that it was the work of the people, by the people, for the people. In other words, personal projects using company equipment and time. In short—stealing.

Adorning Paul concludes the counsel to the slaves of his day by stating the purpose of it: "that they may adorn the doctrine of God our Savior in all things" (Titus 2:10). The Greek word for "adorn" was used of wearing clothes. It was also used of the "setting" of a jewel. The idea is to wear, show off, the doctrine of God our Savior. The doctrine of God refers to the teaching or instruction of God. How you work and relate to your boss can demonstrate what God, your Savior, has taught you. People can see attitudes and actions at work as they relate to work and know God has taught you and are obeying Him.

When people see you at work, what do they see? Do they see a selfish person or the Savior? Does your work manifest your greed or reveal your God?

Your perspective concerning your work determines your attitude toward it. The story is told of men who were working on a building. When one was asked what he was doing, he said,

"Laying bricks." Another said he was making a living for his family, and a third said he was building a cathedral.

Summary: The way to be a Christian employee is to reverently obey and respectfully honor human masters and resist temptations associated with work.

Why do you do a good job? To get paid? To get promoted? To prevent being fired? One company in Cleveland lays it on the line: "We tell our salespeople that if they do a good job, they get to keep it."

According to the New Testament, believers should reverently obey their human masters because the Lord rewards those who do. They should respectfully honor their masters to prevent the Word of God from being blasphemed. They should resist temptation and be loyal employees to adorn God's teaching.

The ultimate issue is to work heartily as unto the Lord. Howard Hendricks talks about being on an American Airlines flight from Boston to Dallas. It was delayed six hours. When the flight finally got underway, a man sitting across from him who soaked up the free booze on every occasion and reamed out the stewardess for the delay. She repeatedly and graciously served him and tried to make his trip as conveniently comfortable as possible. Hendricks went to the galley and said to her, "I am impressed with the way you've handled that man. I would like your name so I can write American Airlines and tell them how much I appreciate your service." She replied, "I appreciate that, but I really don't work for American Airlines; I work for Jesus Christ."

Chapter 8

How To Be A Christian Neighbor

The Bible is a book about relationships. It is primarily about our relationship with the Lord. It also concerns our relationships with our family, fellow believers, and coworkers. Beyond that, it mentions our relationships with those who are not believers.

In the epistles, one of the major passages on the relationship of believers to unbelievers concerns the relationship of a believing wife to an unsaved husband (1 Pet. 3:1-6; see "The Road To The Ultimate in Marriage" course). When the epistles address the relationship between believers and unbelievers, they generally refer to unbelievers as "outside." As applied to unbelievers, it describes them as being without the Lord and outside the faith (Rev. 22:15). Four main passages in the epistles tell believers how to be Christian neighbors to unbelievers.

Do Not Judge Them

Paul says, "But now I have written to you not to keep company with anyone named a brother, who is sexually immoral, or covetous, or an idolater, or a reviler, or a drunkard, or an extortioner; not even to eat with such a person. For what *have* I *to do* with judging those also who are outside? Do you not judge those who are inside? But those who are outside God judges. Therefore put away from yourselves the evil person" (1 Cor. 5:11-13). The point is, "Do not judge unbelievers." To fully understand what Paul is saying, you need to understand the situation in Corinth.

The Situation Paul begins 1 Corinthians 5 by saying, "It is actually reported that there is sexual immorality among you" (1 Cor. 5:1). The term "father's wife" means stepmother. A man in the church was having an affair with a woman who had been or was now married to his father. Paul exclaims not even unsaved people do that! This is a clear-cut case of adultery, which was provable, but the additional factor of it being between a son and a stepmother made it worse. It was a gross sin; it was incest.

The problem was, as Paul says, "And you are puffed up, and have not rather mourned, that he who has done this deed might be taken away from among you" (1 Cor. 5:2). Not only was the man wrong in sinning, but the church was wrong in not dealing with it. That is the problem Paul deals with in this passage.

Paul says they were proud when they should have been mourning that this person might be taken away. He does not say, "You mourn and you do not take away," but mourn *so that* he might be taken away. They were not to do the taking away, which means this does not refer to excommunication.

Although not physically present, Paul has already determined what must be done (1 Cor. 5:3). He says, "In the name of our Lord Jesus Christ when you are gathered together, along with my spirit, with the power of our Lord Jesus Christ, deliver such a one to Satan for the destruction of the flesh, that his spirit may be saved in the day of the Lord Jesus" (1 Cor. 5:4, 5). The Corinthians were to assemble as representatives of Christ by apostolic authority. They were to carry out Paul's decision to deliver such a man to Satan for the destruction of the flesh, that is, for physical death (1 Cor. 11:30; Rom. 8:13; 1 Jn. 5:16; Acts 5:1-11). The purpose was that his spirit might be saved in the day of the Lord Jesus (1 Cor. 5:5), meaning at the Judgment Seat of Christ.

These instructions must be put in context. What Paul commands here is not the first response to a case of gross sin. He had written them before about church discipline (1 Cor. 5:9) and does not repeat all that he had taught them here. From Matthew 18, we know that the sinning brother should be first admonished privately by one person. Then, a small group should see him. It will only be a public issue if he does not respond. The Corinthians followed the procedure until they got to the last step. So, now Paul tells them that by his authority (1 Cor. 5:3, 4), they are to deliver this person to Satan.

From the passages on church discipline, it is evident that the procedure is as follows: 1) there must be a right attitude (1 Cor. 5:2), 2) there must be a right basis; the church must be able to prove the charge objectively (1 Cor. 5:1), and 3) there must be a right process. First, one person goes to the brother, then several, and, finally, the whole church is informed that this brother will not repent, and they are informed not to socialize with him (Mt. 18:15-20; 2 Thess. 3:6-15). That does not mean he is to be treated harshly; instead, he is to be admonished as a brother (see esp. 2 Thess. 3:15).

Perhaps in extreme cases of the grossest sort that causes public scandal, the church should ask God to take that brother home so it can live in peace and purity. There is a sin unto death (Rom. 8:13; 1 Cor. 11:30; Acts 5:1-11; etc.). No doubt God could and would use Satan to accomplish that (Job 1-2; 1 Cor. 5:5).

Paul forthrightly tells them, "Your glorying is not good" (1 Cor. 5:6). The word "glory" should be rendered "boasting." It refers to the subject of their boasting, not the act of boasting. They were proud of their knowledge and wisdom (1 Cor. 1:10-4:21, esp. 3:18 and 4:10). Paul asks, "Do you know that a little leaven leavens the whole lump?" (1 Cor. 5:6). The little leaven of which Paul speaks is not the sinner of verse 1, that is, the person, but the sin, as verse 8 demonstrates. Nor is it the sin of immorality, but the sin of the assembly, namely pride (1 Cor. 5:2) and boasting (1 Cor. 5:6). Sin, like leaven in a lump of dough, will spread until it permeates the whole lump. A tolerated sin will corrupt the whole. That applies to churches as well as individuals.

Paul concludes, "Therefore, purge out the old leaven, that you may be a new lump" (1 Cor. 5:7). The Greek word translated "purge" means "to cleanse thoroughly." They were to cleanse themselves of pride and boasting, symbolically signified here by "old leaven." The purpose of this cleansing is that they might be a new lump without leaven.

The Clarification At this point, Paul clarifies a misunderstanding that resulted from a previous letter he had written to them. He begins by pointing out, "I wrote to you in an epistle not to keep company with sexually immoral people" (1 Cor. 5:9). This statement cannot refer to this epistle because this letter does not contain directions not to keep company with fornicators. Paul is speaking of a previous communication that is now lost. Not all of Paul's writings are extant, but all inspired writings are (Mt. 5:18).

The Greek word translated "to keep company with" denotes living an intimate, continuous relationship with the person. In a former letter, Paul had instructed them not to have such a relationship with an immoral person.

That directive had been misunderstood or misrepresented. So, he clarifies: "Yet I certainly did not mean with the sexually immoral people of this world, or with the covetous, or extortioners, or idolaters, since then you would need to go out of the world" (1 Cor. 5:10). In his earlier epistle, he did not intend to censor contact with gross sinners "of this world," that is, non-Christians. The list of gross sinners includes more than the sexually immoral. It consists of the covetous, those who want more, extortioners, and idolaters. The Greek word "extortioners" means those who seize something and designates those who steal by whatever means.

The reason Paul did not tell believers not to keep company with unbelievers who were gross sinners is that it would be impossible to live, especially in Corinth, without having some contact with them. To not have contact with such non-Christians, a believer would have to live on another planet.

Well, what did Paul mean to say in that prior letter? He explains, "But now I have written to you not to keep company with anyone named a brother, who is a fornicator, or covetous, or an idolater, or a reviler, or a drunkard, or an extortioner—not even to eat with such a person" (1 Cor. 5:11). He has stated what the earlier epistle did not mean (1 Cor. 5:9, 10). Now he states what he did mean (1 Cor. 5:11-13).

The instruction "not to keep company," the same word used in verse 9, was to be applied to anyone named a brother. The apostle adds two more to the list of gross sins given in verse 10. A reviler abuses others. Godet says it speaks rudely, one who calumniates. The drunkard, of course, is the intemperate one with alcohol. With brothers participating in such sins, believers are not to eat, which is not a reference to the Lord's Table, but to ordinary meals (also 1 Thess. 3:14-15).

The reason (see "for" in 5:12) they should have understood his injunction not to keep company with immoral people to apply to a believer is, "For what have I to do with judging those also who are outside? Do you not judge those who are inside? But those who are outside God judges" (1 Cor. 5:12, 13a). God judges unbelievers. Paul has nothing to do with that, but "you," which is emphatic in Greek (1 Cor. 5:12), is said to judge believers. Their responsibility is again made plain.

The conclusion is, "Therefore put away from yourselves that wicked person" (1 Cor. 5:13). This is to be done by delivering the wicked person to Satan (1 Cor. 5:5). The point is that the church should discipline believers who practice open and overt sin, but it should not apply the principle of discipline to unbelievers. Believers should judge that sin is sin, but it is not a believer's job to apply pressure on unbelievers to stop sinning. In that sense, we should not judge unbelievers.

I was playing billiards in a bowling alley with a fellow I had led to the Lord. A fellow repeatedly taking the Lord's name in vain was at the table next to us. The young Christian with me said, "If he does not stop, I will tell him to stop." That is the kind of judging we should not do! The thing to do is befriend the fellow and tell him about the Lord.

Live Godly Before Them

Paul says, "But we urge you, brethren, that you increase more and more; that you also aspire to lead a quiet life, to mind your own business, and to work with your own hands, as we commanded you, that you may walk properly toward those who are outside, and *that* you may lack nothing" (1 Thess. 4:11-12).

The Situation Paul begins by saying, "Finally then, brethren, we urge and exhort in the Lord Jesus that you should abound more and more, just as you received from us how you ought to walk and to please God, for you know what commandments we gave you through the Lord Jesus" (1 Thess. 4:1, 2). The purpose of Paul's appeal is that they would abound more and more in a lifestyle called a walk that is pleasing to the Lord. The question is, of what does such a lifestyle consist?

In the verses that follow, Paul mentions at least three things: 1) Pleasing God means to abound in sexual purity (1 Thess. 4:3-8). 2) Pleasing God means to abound in brotherly love (1 Thess.

4:9-10). Having just said that believers are not to defraud their brothers (1 Thess. 4:6), Paul says believers are to love their brothers (1 Thess. 4:9). 3) Pleasing God means to abound in work (1 Thess. 4:11-12).

The Point The Greek word translated "aspire" (1 Thess. 4:11) means "to strive eagerly or seek earnestly," while "quiet" means "to be still, live quietly, be silent." The concept is to strive to be calm; live a calm, quiet, restful, peaceful life.

Why does Paul bring that up here? Many expositors believe that behind this exhortation was a problem at Thessalonica. Their belief in the imminent return of Christ produced an excitement and a restlessness that was not good; it was a fanatical excitement. Therefore, Paul says, "strive to be calm." This became a problem at Thessalonica, and Paul had to deal with it more directly in a second letter (see 2 Thess. 3:6- 15 in the context of the book of 2 Thess.). Some got so excited over the prospects of the Lord's return that they stopped working. Paul has to tell them to calm down.

He also urges them "to mind your own business" (1 Thess. 4:11b). This should be rendered "practice your own things," that is, be about your personal affairs. They were to love one another (1 Thess. 4:10), but at the same time, they were not to neglect their own personal affairs (1 Thess. 4:11). Again, many commentators feel that Paul is saying this because some of the Thessalonians were becoming meddlesome. What was perhaps a small seed at this point became a full-blown plant later (2 Thess. 3:11). At any rate, Paul says, "Be busy with your own business." In other words, "Don't be a busybody."

Paul adds, "and to work with your own hands, as we commanded you" (1 Thess. 4:11c), an apparent reference to manual labor. This statement has led many to conclude that the church at Thessalonica was blue-collar. Yet, Acts 17:4 seems to indicate a few wealthy converts in the church. The Greeks regarded manual labor as degrading. It was to be performed by slaves. Paul, by example and instruction, underlined the dignity of work.

Paul's purpose in urging them to increase their work was "that you may walk properly toward those who are outside, and that you may lack nothing" (1 Thess. 4:12). The purpose is two-fold. The first is to walk properly, or becomingly, before unbelievers, and the second purpose is that the individual believer lacks nothing.

Abounding in work is becoming a walk with the Lord. Even an unbeliever knows that. God does not want believers to be lazy; He wants them to work. After creating Adam, God's first thing, even before giving him Eve, was to put him to work. So, working is becoming a walk with God. Now Paul says, "Abound in work that you may be becoming in your walk with God before unbelievers."

The point is that believers should have a good testimony among unbelievers. They should be living godly, loving, responsible lives so that will have a good testimony. As Paul told Timothy, an elder "must have a good testimony among those who are outside, lest he fall into reproach and the snare of the devil" (1 Tim. 3:7).

Will Rogers once said, "What this country needs is dirtier fingernails and cleaner minds." Paul would echo that sentiment and add a loving heart. When you were a child, there were those times your mother told you to clean up, get dressed, and report for inspection. When you returned, she would look you over and say things like, "Let me see your hands. Did you brush your teeth? Is your hair combed?" When satisfied, she would smile and say, "Now sit down and wait until we're ready to go." If God, like our mothers, called us in for inspection, for what would He look? What would it take to get that smile of approval? This passage leads us to the conclusion that the answer is a clean mind, a loving heart, and dirty fingernails!

Serve Them

Do Good Paul says, "And let us not grow weary while doing good, for in due season we shall reap if we do not lose heart. Therefore as we have the opportunity, let us do good to all, especially to those who are of the household of faith" (Gal. 6:9-10). The good that Paul has in mind is that which is beneficial and beautiful. The Greek word translated "good" in Galatians 6:9 means that which is good primarily in outward form, fair, beautiful, whereas the word for good in verse 10 signifies that which is right, beneficial.

Be Ready The good works are to be done as an opportunity comes. Some people have more opportunities than others do. Some situations provide more opportunities than others do. Sometimes, there are more opportunities than at other times. Every believer should be ready for every good work (Titus 3:1).

Furthermore, these good works should be done for all. The "all" of Galatians may even include the Judaizers, but it certainly includes non-Christians because the "all" is in contrast to believers.

One expression of love is serving people (Gal. 5:13), all people, believers, and unbelievers alike. Service can be exhausting (Gal. 6:9). The loving servant can get tired and become discouraged. He can relax his effort, slack off, and give up. Paul says do not do that. Remember the law of the harvest. It's not the reaper who decides the kind and size of the harvest; it is the sower.

So, be ready to do good to unbelieving neighbors. Be respectful. Don't mow the lawn before nine on Saturday morning. Collect the mail and the newspapers when they are out of town.

Someone has written, "My life shall touch a dozen lives before this day is done; leave countless marks for good or ill, ere sets the evening sun. This is the wish I always wish, the prayer I always pray: Lord, may my life help other lives it touches."

Give Them the Gospel

Paul says, "Walk in wisdom toward those *who are* outside, redeeming the time" (Col. 4:5). In a sense, Colossians 4:2-6 consists of three general exhortations. A careful analysis of these verses, however, indicates that these three exhortations, one way or another, touch on the believer's relationship to the unsaved world, and beyond that, all three injunctions concern evangelism. Therefore, these verses tell believers three things to do to win someone to Christ.

Pray with Thanksgiving Paul says, "Continue earnestly in prayer, being vigilant in it with thanksgiving" (Col. 4:2). The word translated "earnestly" means "to be awake." It was used figuratively to mean being alive and alert. Paul is saying, "Wake up. Watch out. Be alert. Concentrate." This prayer is to be "with thanksgiving."

After exhorting the believers at Colosse to pray in general, Paul entreats them to pray specifically for him. He asks for two things (see the two "thats," one in verse 3 and the other in verse 4). First, he desires that they would pray that he will have an opportunity to witness. He says, "Meanwhile praying also for us, that God would open to us a door for the word, to speak the mystery of Christ, for which I am also in chains" (Col. 4:3). The phrase "open to us a door" means "to give us an opportunity."

Paul desired an opportunity to speak the Word. That includes preaching the gospel, but it is more. The "Word" is further defined as "the mystery of Christ," which has been revealed about Christ. Earlier in the book, he spoke of the mystery God wanted him to make known. He described it as "Christ in you, the hope of glory" (Col. 1:27). In the book of Ephesians, which further elaborates on this mystery, Paul defines it as Jews and Gentiles being members of the same body.

Paul's second prayer request was "that I may make it manifest, as I ought to speak" (Col. 4:4). Opportunity was his immediate purpose; boldness was his ultimate purpose. It is one thing for God to open a door; it is another for the believer to enter it. The place to begin evangelism is to pray for an opportunity and for the openness and boldness to seize it.

Walk with Wisdom Paul commands, "Walk in wisdom toward those who are outside, redeeming the time" (Col. 4:5). Those who are "outside" are those outside of Christ. Believers are to conduct themselves in such a wise way that their lives will attract, impress, and convict the non-Christians around them. The story is told of an over-zealous Christian who approached a Jewish rabbi and asked, "Sir, when are Jews going to become Christians?" The rabbi replied, "The Jews will become Christians when the Christians become Christians."

Part of walking in wisdom before non-Christians is "redeeming the time." The Greek word "time" refers to "a point of time, a time for some given action, significant time, an opportunity." In other words, this is saying, "Buy up opportunities. Let no opportunity slip past you without saying and doing what may further the cause of Christ." Purchase and seize every opportunity. Take every opportunity to live to attract the unsaved.

Speak with Grace Paul's third command is, "Let your speech always be with grace, seasoned with salt, that you may know how you ought to answer each one" (Col. 4:6). A wise walk must be followed by a witness of the spoken word. The phrase "with grace" can refer to the giver, that is, he is to be gracious, kind, expressing goodwill, or it can describe that which causes favorable regard, acceptableness, pleasingness, charming pleasantness, attractiveness, winsomeness. Eadie says, "It is that gracious spirit which rules the tongue and prompts it both to select a fitting theme and to clothe them in the most agreeable and impressive forms."

This gracious and winsome speech must be seasoned with salt. Salt does two things: 1) it preserves from corruption and renders wholesome, and 2) it gives flavor and recommends to the taste. The latter meaning seems to be the idea here, as "seasoned" indicates. The concept is more of winsomeness than wholesomeness.

In their zeal for evangelism, some are curt, caustic, and sarcastic. They need to talk with tenderness, not toughness in their voice. Believers can be bold and harsh, tactless, and even rude. Or, they can be bold and, at the same time, be skillful, smooth, tasteful, and tactful. If we are to win some, we must be winsome.

Paul adds, "That you may know how you ought to answer each one" (Col. 4:6b). This is the purpose of speaking with grace seasoned with salt. Of course, believers should always speak with grace, but Paul specifically applies it to talking to unbelievers. If believers practiced "grace of speech," it would not "desert them" when defending their beliefs suddenly confronted them.

Believers need to know how to reply to each individual. The same answer will not do in every case. Their conversation must be appropriate for and exactly adapted to the individual. Chrysostom said, "A prince must be answered one way, and a subject another; a rich man one way, and a poor man another."

A godly walk will provoke questions (1 Pet. 3:15). What believers say in response is important, but how they say it is equally important. In Colossians 4:6, Paul is talking about speaking graciously and being winsome. In 2 Timothy 2:24, he says, "Be gentle, be warm." Believers should not offend or be offensive, but the reality is that no matter how tasteful and tactful they are, the gospel offends some people. The Scripture teaches there is an offense of the cross.

Summary: The way to be a Christian neighbor is not to judge unbelievers but to live godly lives before them, do good things for them, and give them the gospel.

The religious leaders of Jesus' day tried to trap Him. They sent a lawyer to ask Him what the greatest commandment is (Mt. 22:34-36). He responded, "You shall love the LORD your God with all your heart, with all your soul, and with all your mind. This is *the* first and great commandment. And *the* second *is* like it: 'You shall love your neighbor as yourself'" (Mt. 22:27-39). If we love God, we are to love our neighbor (1 Jn. 3:10-18; 4:7-21). As one commentator said, "Our neighbor's interest must be as dear to us as our own" (Plummer).

Someone has said:

People are illogical, unreasonable, and self-centered.
   Love them anyway.
If you do good, people will accuse you of selfish motives.
   Do good anyway.
If you are successful, you win false friends and true enemies.
   Succeed anyway.
The good you do today will be forgotten tomorrow.
   Do good anyway.
Honesty and frankness make you vulnerable.
   Be honest and frank anyway.
People favor underdogs but follow only top dogs.
   Fight for a few underdogs anyway.

What you spend years building may be destroyed overnight. Build anyway.

People really need help but may attack you if you do help them. Help them anyway.

Give the world the best you have and you'll get kicked in the teeth. Give the world the best you have anyway.

Chapter 9

How To Be A Christian Citizen

Someone has written, "I have been a travel agent for thirty years. The following are examples of why our country is in trouble!

"I had a New Hampshire Congresswoman ask for an aisle seat so that her hair wouldn't get messed up by being near the window.

"I got a call from a candidate's staffer who wanted to go to Capetown. I started explaining the flight length and the passport information when she interrupted me with, 'I'm not trying to make you look stupid, but Capetown is in Massachusetts.' Without trying to make her look stupid, I calmly explained, 'Cape Cod is in Massachusetts, Capetown is in Africa.' Her response—click.

"A senior Vermont Congressman called, furious about a Florida package we did. I asked what was wrong with the vacation in Orlando. He said he was expecting an ocean view room. I tried to explain that it's impossible since Orlando is in the middle of the state. He replied, 'Don't lie to me. I looked on the map and Florida is a very thin state!'

"I got a call from a lawmaker's wife who asked, 'Is it possible to see England from Canada?' I said, 'No.' She said, 'But they look so close on the map.'

"An aide for a Bush cabinet member once called and asked if he could rent a car in Dallas. When I pulled up the reservation, I noticed he had only a 1-hour layover in Dallas. When I asked him why he wanted to rent a car, he said, 'I heard Dallas was a big airport, and we will need a car to drive between gates to save time.'

"An Illinois Congresswoman called last week. She needed to know how it was possible that her flight from Detroit left at 8:30 am and got to Chicago at 8:33 am. I explained that Michigan was an hour ahead of Illinois, but she couldn't understand the concept of time zones. Finally, I told her the plane was a jet and went very fast; she bought that.

"A Georgia lawmaker called and asked, 'Do airlines put your physical description on your bag, so they know whose luggage belongs to whom?' I said, 'No, why do you ask?' She replied, 'Well, when I checked in with the airline, they put a tag on my luggage that said (FAT), and I'm overweight. I think that's very rude!' After putting her on hold for a minute while I looked into it (I was laughing), I came back and explained the city code for Fresno, CA, is FAT, and the airline was just putting a destination tag on her luggage.

"A Senator's aide called to inquire about a trip package to Hawaii. After going over all the cost info, she asked, 'Would it be cheaper to fly to California and then take the train to Hawaii?'

"I just got off the phone with a freshman Congressman who asked, 'How do I know which plane to get on?' I asked him what exactly he meant, to which he replied, 'I was told my flight number is 823, but none of these darn planes have numbers on them.'

"A lady Senator called and said, 'I need to fly to Pepsi-Cola, Florida. Do I have to get on one of those little computer planes?' I asked if she meant to fly on a commuter plane to Pensacola, Fl. She said, 'Yeah, whatever!'

"A senior California Senator called and had a question about the documents he needed to fly to China. After a lengthy discussion about passports, I reminded him he needed a visa. 'Oh, no, I don't. I've been to China many times and never had to have one of those.' I double-checked and sure enough, his stay required a visa. When I told him this, he said, 'Look, I've been to China four times, and they have accepted my American Express every time!'

"A New Mexico Congresswoman called to make reservations, 'I want to go from Chicago to Rhino, New York.' The agent was at a loss for words. Finally, the agent said, 'Are you sure that's the town's name?' 'Yes, what flights do you have?' replied the lady. After some searching, the agent returned with, 'I'm sorry, ma'am, I've looked up every airport code in the country and can't find a Rhino anywhere.' The lady retorted, 'Oh, don't be silly! Everyone knows where it is. Check your map!" The agent scoured a map of the state of New York and finally offered, 'You don't mean Buffalo, do you?' 'That's it! I knew it was a big animal,' she said."

The piece ended with, "Now you know why Government is in the shape it's in." Perhaps such a list can be assembled for any occupation. Not all government workers are that dumb, but such experiences shape our attitude toward government.

What should our attitude be? What do believers have to do to be Christian citizens? When believers in Jesus Christ take their Christianity seriously, they ask, "What does it mean to be a Christian husband or wife, a Christian parent, a Christian employer or employee, a Christian neighbor?" Eventually, they will ask, "What does it mean to be a Christian citizen?"

Pray

The first thing believers should do to be Christian citizens is to pray for those in authority.

The Plan "Therefore I exhort first of all that supplications, prayers, intercessions, *and* giving of thanks be made for all men" (1 Tim. 2:1). Paul exhorts the men in the church assembly to pray (1 Tim. 2:8). The Greek word translated "supplications" means "a need, an asking" (A-S). It comes from a verb that means "to lack" and denotes prayer that springs from a sense of need. The Greek word for "prayers" is the most general word for prayer to God. As compared to supplication, which is a prayer regarding a specific situation, "prayers" refers to requests that are always present, such as the need for more wisdom. Intercession is prayer for others. All this is to be done for all with thanksgiving. No racial, political, economic, or social class is excluded.

Prayer for all includes prayer "for kings and all who are in authority" (1 Tim. 2:2a). The "kings" of today are the presidents and prime ministers. These prayers are not limited to the supreme rulers but include all who are in authority, which would consist of

Congress, the Supreme Court, and state and local officials in the USA. Don't forget police officers and firemen.

The Purpose Paul gives two purposes for praying. The first concerns believers and the second concerns the gospel's spread.

The first purpose is "that we may lead a quiet and peaceable life in all godliness and reverence" (1 Tim. 2:2b). The purpose is not that political leaders might lead a godly life, but that believers might ("we"). The government is to achieve peace and security conditions so believers can pursue their lives. Freedom from war and persecution facilitates the spread of the gospel.

Four words describe the kind of life Paul wants believers to live. Quiet and peaceable indicate the absence of war, anarchy, and persecution. This tranquil life is to be lived "in all godliness and reverence." Some say these two words describe the believer's relationship with God and others. Believers are to be reverent toward God and have a serious approach toward life that commands respect for others.

Paul explains the second purpose of prayer: "For this *is* good and acceptable in the sight of God our Savior, who desires all men to be saved and to come to the knowledge of the truth" (1 Tim. 2:3-4). Prayer for all is "good and acceptable in the sight of God" because God desires all to be saved. The ultimate purpose of these prayers is that people be saved. Praying for those in authority so that there may be peace will enable the gospel to spread. The book of Acts records, "Then the churches throughout all Judea, Galilee, and Samaria had peace and were edified. And walking in the fear of the Lord and in the comfort of the Holy Spirit, they were multiplied" (Acts 9:31).

Jesus says, "Is it not written, 'My house shall be called a house of prayer for all nations'? But you have made it a 'den of thieves'" (Mk. 11:17). Churches today are known for their Pastor or their music or programs. Imagine a church being known as a place of prayer for all nations. That may be hard for us to imagine today, but that was what Jesus said should happen.

Submit

The Responsibility Paul pens, "Let every soul be subject to the governing of authorities" (Rom. 13:1a). "Every soul" is to subject himself or herself to government. In Roman society, there were three levels of people: slaves who had no rights, the rank and file who had little voice in government but a heavy load of government, and the privileged elite. Paul says every soul, not just every citizen, in the country, is to submit to every level of government. The Greek word translated "be subject" was a military term that means "to place or rank under," "to subject oneself, to obey."

The Reason Why should believers submit themselves to the government? In what follows, Paul gives several reasons to submit to the government.

1. Philosophically, because God has ordained government. Paul explains, "For there is no authority except from God, and the authorities that exist are appointed by God" (Rom. 13:1b). There is no authority God has not permitted to exist (Dan. 2:21, 37; 4:17, 32; 5:21). Thus, the reason to submit to government is

that government is ordained by God.

Paul concludes, "Therefore, whoever resists the authority resists the ordinance of God" (Rom. 13:2a). If God appoints civil authority, it logically follows that to resist the authority is to resist a divinely appointed arrangement. This statement contains two different Greek words for resist. The first means "to set oneself against, to rage and battle against," while the second means "to withstand, oppose." Resistance includes crime and illegal activity, as well as rebellion and revolution.

Paul adds, "And those who resist will bring judgment to themselves" (Rom. 13:2b). The one who is ultimately being resisted is God, who will judge such rebellion, which will probably come through human authorities.

2. Practically, because government has the power to punish. Paul continues, "For rulers are not a terror to good works, but to evil. Do you want to be unafraid of the authority? Do what is good, and you will have praise from the same. For he is God's minister to you for good. But if you do evil, be afraid; for he does not bear the sword in vain; for he is God's minister, an avenger to execute wrath on him who practices evil" (Rom. 13:3-4). Government is to be obeyed because it is appointed to punish evil and promote good.

God ordained government to punish evil. If you do evil, as in resisting the laws of government, you should fear because government is God's servant to execute wrath on evildoers. Government has the divine right to bear a sword, the instrument of death. War and capital punishment are included. The common method of capital punishment in Paul's day was decapitation with a sword.

God ordains government to promote good. Twice in these two verses, Paul refers to government as God's ministers, that is, God's servants. Government is God's servant to praise those who do well.

Government has the right and the responsibility to maintain an army, a police department, and a court system. The Constitution of the United States puts it like this: "To provide for the common defense, promote the general welfare, and ensure domestic tranquility." The government is to protect the community from within and without and punish criminals.

We are to obey the law for fear of getting caught. We are to pay taxes to keep from going to jail. We ought to keep the speed limit to prevent getting a ticket.

3. Personally, because you have a conscience. A man wrote to the IRS, saying, "A few years ago, I cheated on my income tax. My conscience has been troubling me and I haven't been able to sleep, so I enclose a check for $50.00. If I can't sleep, I'll send you the rest."

Paul is not suggesting that we only submit to the government for fear of punishment. To clarify, he concludes by saying, "Therefore you must be subject, not only because of wrath but also for conscience's sake" (Rom. 13:5). Granted, we ought to obey the government so we will not be punished, but also because it is our spiritual duty before God. The unbeliever fulfills his obligation to the state for fear of punishment, perhaps because he knows the government is to benefit society. The believer has another motivation as well, namely, the Lord. The external motive is wrath; the internal motive is the will of God.

We are to pay taxes not because the IRS might audit us but because God will audit us. We are to keep the speed limit not because we see the policeman but because we see the Lord and the Lord sees us.

The Result Paul has spoken generally. Now he gets more specific: "For because of this, you also pay taxes, for they are God's ministers attending continually to this very thing" (Rom. 13:6). Believers submit to the government and pay taxes because it is the will of God.

Paul concludes, "Render therefore to all their due: taxes to whom taxes are due, customs to whom customs, fear to whom fear, honor to whom honor" (Rom. 13:7). The believer's obligation to government is broader than taxes. They are to pay various forms of taxes and give officials personal respect.

As Donald Gray Barnhouse wrote, "I buy gasoline and pay its taxes, thankful for the fine roads over which I drive. I enjoy the beauty of a national park paid for by our taxes. I see our lighthouses or the tail of a jet plane, and I'm grateful for the forces that guard our coast and defend our skies" (Barnhouse, p. 123).

Honor

Agreement with Paul Peter says, "Therefore submit yourselves to every ordinance of man for the Lord's sake, whether to the King as supreme or to governors" (1 Pet. 2:13-14a). Some of what Peter says about the believer's relationship to government overlaps what Paul says in Romans 13 and Titus 3:1.

Peter and Paul are agreed that believers are to submit. They are to voluntarily submit to "every ordinance of man," that is, every institution founded and formed by men, not necessarily explicitly established by God. The expression "for the Lord's sake" can mean 1) out of regard for His authority or 2) out of concern for His cause (1 Pet. 2:15-16). There is obedience because of duty and there is obedience out of devotion. Believers are to submit to supreme rulers and to subordinate government officials. They are to obey all levels of government, from the traffic court to the Supreme Court, from city hall to the halls of Congress.

Peter and Paul agree that the government should punish evildoers and praise those who do good. Peter adds, "as to those who are sent by him for the punishment of evildoers and for the praise of those who do good" (1 Pet. 2:14b). The purpose of government is to punish vice and praise virtue.

Peter and Paul agree that believers are to submit to government because it is the will of God. Peter explains, "For this is the will of God, that by doing good you may put to silence the ignorance of foolish men" (1 Pet. 2:15). Earlier, Peter pointed out that the reason for submission to the government was "for the Lord's sake" (1 Pet. 1:13). He now says it is the will of God. Paul elaborates on this concept (Rom. 13:1-7). Peter traces the practical result of submission to the government. By doing good, the believer will "put to silence the ignorance of foolish men."

Peter inserts a personal reminder to believers: "as free yet not using your liberty as a cloak for vice, but as servants of God" (1 Pet. 2:16). Spiritually, believers are free, free from sin (Jn. 8:36) and free from the Mosaic Law (Gal. 5:1, 13). Their freedom from sin, however, was not to be used as a veil for vice. The word translated "vice" occurs in 1 Pet. 2:1, where it was rendered "malice." Here, it is used in the general sense of wickedness. Christian freedom is not a license to practice wickedness. It is the freedom to be a slave of God. As a slave of God, believers will submit to government because it is God's will.

In addition to Paul Peter concludes this paragraph with a list of specifics. "Honor all people, love the brotherhood, fear God, honor the king" (1 Pet. 2:17). Four commands are issued, consisting of two couplets. In the first couplet, general respect for all men is deepened to love for the brotherhood. In the second couplet, the fear of God is extended to honoring the King. Paul says believers are to render honor to whom honor is due (Rom. 13:7). Peter is specific. He says, "Honor the king."

Peter began by saying, "Honor all." He concludes with, "Honor the king." Peter has put the emperor on the same level as all people. Contrary to the claims of Roman emperors, they are not equal to God. Believers have obligations to the state, but their obligations to God and to the brotherhood are higher.

Government is to be obeyed, and the governor is to be honored, but government is not to be obeyed above God, and governors are to be honored like all other men. Honor to all, especially the king, love for believers, and fear toward God are good works which will silence the slander of sinister, sinful men. The king is not necessarily honored and certainly not feared as a god, but he is to be honored, that is, respected.

The subject of submission to government raises some questions, such as, what if the ruler is evil? Is this submission absolute? And how does this apply to a democracy?

Submission is not conditioned upon the righteousness of the ruler. Christ called a ruler, Herod, a fox (Lk. 13:32), but He did not resist Herod's authority. To avoid anarchy, some form of government is needed in a greater or lesser degree. A bad government is better than no government.

When Peter wrote these words, the king was Nero, who reigned from AD 54 to 68 and under whose persecution Peter himself would later be put to death. He was an ungodly and unrighteous man. He was a cruel, vicious, amoral tyrant. Nero came to the throne because his mother, Agrippina, scratched to get him there, pushing aside the son of Claudius, the legal heir. Her son rewarded her by having her banished and murdered. He also killed Claudius' son, who was still the heir apparent. The personal character of the officeholder does not release the believer from obeying the king.

Defense counsel at the Nuremberg trials argued that the Nazi leaders who killed over 6 million Jews had done so in obedience to their governments, but the court found them guilty because they should have disobeyed the government in obedience to a higher law, that of humane treatment for their fellow man.

How To Be A Christian Citizen

Submission to authority is not absolute because the authority God has given is not unlimited. Sometimes, a believer must obey God rather than man (Acts 4:19, 5:29). Believers are to obey, except when commanded to sin (Grudem). "Civil disobedience may occur only when rulers acting on purely human authority *require* Christians to sin" (Adams). This, however, does not warrant all civil disobedience. Apart from being forced to sin, civil disobedience by believers cannot be justified by the Scripture.

As for submission in a democracy, "To prevent abuses of God's purpose for government, it is right for Christians to pray and work for governments that act according to God's will (1 Tim. 2:1-4; Ps. 82:1-4; 125:3)" (Grudem). Barclay says, "In a democratic state, the keynote must not be *subjection*, but *cooperation*, for in a democratic state, the duty of the citizen is not only to submit to the ruler but to take the necessary share in ruling. Hence, if the Christian is to fulfill his duty to the state, he must take part in the government of the state."

When the government prohibits something God Himself commands or the law of our land commands something God prohibits and believers are forced to disobey, they must do so respectfully. Instead of calling the IRS the "Infernal Revenue Service" or the "Eternal Revenue Service," believers should honor the government and cheerfully pay their taxes. Jokes about politicians are often harmless, but sometimes, I wonder if they do cross the line into disrespect. Indeed, outright lies and defamation of character should not be among believers, no matter how strong their political feelings.

Summary: The way to be a Christian citizen is to pray for government leaders, submit to them, and honor them.

Christians have dual citizenship: one in Heaven (Phil. 3:20) and one on earth. The Pharisees sent their disciples with the Herodians to ask the Lord, "Tell us, therefore, what do You think? Is it lawful to pay taxes to Caesar, or not?" (Mt. 22:17). Jesus asked them to show Him a coin and asked, 'Whose image and inscription *is* this?' (Mt. 22:20). They said to Him, 'Caesar's.'" (Mt. 22:21a). "And He said to them, 'Render therefore to Caesar the things that are Caesar's, and to God the things that are God's'" (Mt. 22:21b). The Greek word translated "render" means "to give back, restore, return, to render" what is due, "to pay." When they asked the question, they used a word for giving (see "pay" in Mt. 22:17) as though a gift might be withheld (McNeile). Jesus uses a word ("render") that indicates the tax was a "moral obligation" (Plummer; Toussaint).

In other words, He instructed them "not to *give* tribute to Caesar, but to *give back* to Caesar what belongs to him and, at the same time, to give back to God what belonged to God" (Tasker). Jesus is saying that if they enjoyed the benefits of government, they should pay the taxes owed as well as give God what belonged to Him (Toussaint). Taxes are not a gift but a debt for benefits received (Tasker).

Commenting on the incident in the Lord's life when He paid the Temple tax (Mt. 17:24-27), Barclay says, "This story was put into the Gospels to tell Christians, especially the Jewish Christians, that, however unpleasant they might be, the duties of the citizen must be shouldered and accepted. This story is told to tell us that Christianity and good citizenship go hand in hand. The Christian who exempts himself from the duties of good citizenship is not only failing in citizenship; he is also failing in Christianity."

Since Caesar's image is on the coin, they should pay back to Caesar what is his, and since God's image is on man (Gen. 1:26-27), they should give to God what bears His image, namely, themselves.

If you are giving to God what belongs to Him, you will give to Caesar what belongs to him.

BIBLIOGRAPHY

Abbott-Smith, G. *A Manual Greek Lexicon of the New Testament*. Edinburgh: T & T. Clark. 1960.

Adams, Jay E. *Trust and Obey*. Phillipsburg, New Jersey: Presbyterian and Reform Publishing Co., 1980.

Barclay, William. *The Letters of James and Peter*. Philadelphia: The Westminster Press, 1960.

Barclay, William. *The Gospel of Matthew*, vol. 1. Philadelphia: The Westminster Press, 1958.

Barclay, William. *The Gospel of Matthew*, vol. 2. Philadelphia: The Westminster Press, 1958.

Barclay, William. *The Letters to Philippians, Colossians, and Thessalonians,* Philadelphia: The Westminster Press, 1959.

Barclay, William. *More New Testament Words*. New York: Harper & Row, Publishers, 1958.

Bits and Pieces, December 1989.

Bits and Pieces, October 1990.

Bits and Pieces, October 15, 1992.

Bruce, F. F. *The Book of Acts*, The New Testament Commentary on the New Testament. Grand Rapids: William B. Eerdmans Publishing Company, 1989.

Bruce, F. F. *The Epistle to the Ephesians*. London: Pickering & Inglis, LTD., 1968.

Crabb, Lawrence and Allender, Don B. *Encouragement*. Grand Rapids: Zondervan Publishing House, 1984.

Crabb, Lawrence. *The Marriage Builder*. Grand Rapids: Zondervan Publishing House, 1992.

Eadie, John. *Commentary on the Epistle to the Colossians*. Grand Rapids: Zondervan Publishing House, 1957 reprint of the 1856 edition.

Eadie, John. *Commentary on the Epistle to the Ephesians*. Grand Rapids: Zondervan Publishing House, reprint of the 1883 edition.

Erdman, Charles R. *The Epistle of Paul to the Ephesians*. Philadelphia: The Westminster Press, 1974.

Fitzgerald, Ernest. *Keeping Pace*. Greensboro: Pace Communications Inc., 1988.

Hiebert, D. Edmond. *First Timothy*. Chicago: Moody Press, 1957.

Hoehner, Harold W. *Ephesians: an Exegetical Commentary*. Grand Rapids: Baker Academic, 2006.

Mains, Karen Burton. *Open Heart/Open Home*. Downers Grove, Ill.: InterVarsity Press, 2002.

M'Neile, Alan Hugh. *The Gospel According to St. Matthew*. London: Macmillan and Company, 1961.

Marshall, I. Howard. *Acts*, Tyndale New Testament Commentaries. Grand Rapids: William B. Eerdmans, 1986.

Moulton, James Hope and Milligan, George. *The Vocabulary of the Greek Testament*. Grand Rapids: Wm. B. Eerdmans Publishing Company, 1972.

Godet, F. *Commentary on the First Epistle of St. Paul to the Corinthians*. Grand Rapids: Zondervan Publishing House, 1957 reprint of the 1886 edition.

Bibliography

Gromacki, Robert G. *Stand True to the Charge, An Exposition of 1 Timothy*. Schaumburg, Ill.: Regular Baptist Press, 1982.

Grudem, Wayne. *The First Epistle of Peter*, Tyndale New Testament Commentaries. Grand Rapids: Eerdmans Publishing Company, 1988.

Guthrie, Donald. *The Pastoral Epistles*, The Tyndale New Testament Commentaries. Grand Rapids: William B. Eerdmans Publishing Company, 1986.

Hendriksen, William. *A Commentary on I & II Timothy and Titus*, London: The Banner of Truth Trust, 1964.

Hodge, Charles. *A Commentary on the Epistle to the Ephesians*. London: The Banner of Truth Trust, 1964 reprint of the 1856 edition.

Hodge, Charles. *Commentary on the Epistles to the Romans*. Grand Rapids: William B. Eerdmans Publishing Company, 1976 reprint of the 1886 edition.

Kent Jr., Homer A. *The Pastoral Epistle*. Chicago: Moody Press, 1966.

Plummer, Alfred. *An Exegetical Commentary of the Gospel According to St. Matthew*. Minneapolis: James Family Christian Publishers, ND.

Plummer, Alfred. *The Pastoral Epistles*. London: Hodder and Stoughton, 1888.

Rackham, Richard Belward, *The Acts of the Apostle*. London: Methuen & Co. LTD., the 1957 reprint of the 1901 edition.

Reader's Digest, December 1981.

Robinson, J. Armitage. *St. Paul's Epistle to the Ephesians.* London: James Clarke & Co. LTD., N. D.

Stibbs, A. M. and Walls, A. F. *The First Epistle of Peter*, Tyndale New Testament Commentaries. Grand Rapids: William B. Eerdmans Publishing Company, 1983.

Grudem, Wayne. *The First Epistle of Peter*, Tyndale New Testament Commentaries. Grand Rapids: William B. Eerdmans Publishing Company, 1988.

Tasker, R. V. G. *Matthew,* The Tyndale New Testament Commentaries. Grand Rapids: William B. Eerdmans Publishing Company, 1961.

Toussaint, Stanley D. *Behold the King.* Portland, OR: Multnomah Press, 1980.

Trench, Richard Chenevix, *Synonyms of the New Testament.* Grand Rapids: Eerdmans, 1963.

Westcott, Brooke Foss. *Saint Paul's Epistle to the Ephesians.* Minneapolis: Klock & Klock Christian Publishers, 1978 reprint of the 1906 edition.

Wiersbe, Warren W. *Be Rich.* Wheaton, IL: Victor Books, 1984.

Washington, Booker T. *Up from Slavery.* New York: Doubleday, 1901.

About The Author

G. Michael Cocoris is a gifted communicator. He can make even complicated subjects simple, clear, and practical. His breadth of experience has allowed him to relate to a wide range of audiences.

Michael received a Bachelor of Arts degree from Tennessee Temple University, a Master of Theology degree from Dallas Seminary, and a Doctorate of Divinity from Biola University. He traveled the United States for over a dozen years as a speaker. He has also been a seminary professor, visiting lecturer, and world traveler, including hosting tours to Israel and China.

Michael has pastored three churches, including a rural church when he was in seminary, an urban church, the historic Church of the Open Door, first in downtown Los Angeles and later in Glendora, California, and a suburban church, the Lindley Church in Tarzana California, a suburb of Los Angeles. While at the Church of Open Door, he had a daily radio broadcast.

Michael has written numerous magazine articles, mainly for *Biblical Research Monthly*. He has authored a number of books, including *Seventy Years on Hope Street, A History of the Church of the Open Door*; *How To Live A Biblical Spiritual Life, Clarifying the Confusion*; *Repentance, The Most Misunderstood Word in the Bible*; *Evangelism: A Biblical Approach*; *The Salvation Controversy*; *Lordship Salvation: Is It Biblical?*; *The Books of the Bible, the Subject, Structure, Situation, and Significant Verses of Each Book*; *Psalms, A Song for Every Situation, Each Summarized on One Page*; and *Counseling Theories, A Biblical Evaluation*. In addition, he was a contributor to The *NKJV Study Bible* and *Nelson's New Illustrated Bible Commentary*.

Michael is the pastor of the Lindley Church in Tarzana, California. He and his wife, Patricia, live in Santa Monica, California. See Mike's website at *www.insightsfromtheword.com*.

www.ingramcontent.com/pod-product-compliance
Lightning Source LLC
Chambersburg PA
CBHW070109080526
44586CB00013B/1238